MAGIC CARPET RIDE
NIALL QUINN

The story of
Niall Quinn's time at
Sunderland AFC

MAGIC CARPET RIDE
NIALL QUINN

The story of Niall Quinn's time at Sunderland AFC

SEVEN7Y3

Produced by the writing team of Seventy3 Magazine

DB PUBLISHING

This edition published in Great Britain in 2013 by DB Publishing, an imprint of JMD Media.

Cover Design: Andrew Brewster

Disclaimer: All views expressed within these pages are that of the author and do not always represent the views of Seventy3 magazine or Media73 Ltd.

ISBN 9781780912066

Printed and bound by Copytech (UK) Limited, Peterborough.

Contents

Chapter Breakdown

Author's Note – Prologue to the book

Foreword by former Sunderland player – KEVIN PHILLIPS

Niall Quinn Timeline of events

1. The Indian Summer – A recap of Quinn's illustrious playing career in particular his time at Sunderland in which he scored a winner versus arch rivals Newcastle, gave away his testimonial proceeds to charity, endearing himself to the North East region. **MAL ROBINSON**

2. Quinn's Return – Summer 2006 and the return of the great man to the club as Chairman and head of the Drumaville consortium featuring an interview with Charlie Chawke one of the members and quotes and stories from Quinn himself from that time. **CHRIS O HARA**

3. Niall Quinn – The Manager – A candid look back at Quinn's time spent in charge of the team when involved in the dual role of Chairman and Manager at a football club and the disastrous run which led to a new era at the club. **GARY EMMERSON**

4. The Irish Revolution – The arrival of Roy Keane at the club and the consequent arrival of new players and promotion back to the Premier League from the bottom of the league table, looking at Quinn's interjection with the fans that season winning them back via a series of supporter talk-in nights. **ANDY POWELL AND JIM FOX**

5. Black Cat Down – A chapter dedicated to the extraordinary story of when a football chairman paid for 80 stranded Sunderland fans to travel from Bristol to the North East in a fleet of taxis. Featuring quotes, comments and eye witness accounts. **JIM FOX**

In memory of Trevor 'Oz' Oswald.
SAFC through and through 1962-2013.

Author's Note

Niall Quinn won't thank us for writing this book. Not because of personal invasion or publishing any inflammatory revelations as that is not what the book is about, not that Quinny a devoted family man would probably have any anyway!

The reason Niall Quinn won't like us for writing this book is because he is probably the most modest man in football and he would simply say he was doing a job for the club, his club and the City of Sunderland, his adopted City.

As is further detailed within the book, Niall Quinn arrived at Sunderland AFC a gangly striker gambled on to help keep the club in the Premier League in its first season there in 1996 at Roker Park. Fifteen years later, he left the Stadium of Light (albeit with a four year gap between 2002 and 2006) an established Premier League side, now looking for the next step up to the possibilities of European football, not seen on Wearside since 1973.

In his time he has been player, manager and chairman, not to mention responsible for international development, scoring the winner in a North-east Derby against arch rivals Newcastle United, which guarantees legendary status alone, not forgetting donating proceeds from his testimonial (between Sunderland and the Republic of Ireland national side) to Sunderland and Dublin's Children's hospitals.

His outstanding contribution though to the football club will be seen as the one he made in 2006 when putting together a consortium comprising of Irish and local businessmen, he saved Sunderland from what could have been catastrophic consequences, which if allowed to proceed could have certainly ended in tears and meltdown for football in the red and white strongholds of the North East.

As Editor-in-Chief for *Seventy3* Magazine, I have the pleasure of meeting a realm of former and current stars for Sunderland and in football in general. Launched in March 2011 and slowly becoming established in the area around the summer of the same year, we perhaps missed out on the opportunity to form any relationship with Niall Quinn, as the big man stepped aside as Chairman, handing over the reigns to Ellis Short, before embarking on his overseas role for the club, subsequent to severing his red and white ties altogether.

I had met Niall a number of times face to face, more so on hospitality events and long before *Seventy3* began and more an excuse to be on a photograph – one of thousands the big man must have been asked to smile on at a typical matchday and which must have been so easily forgettable for Wearside's favourite Irishman.

I though do have a slight claim to fame in association with Niall Quinn. It was whilst producing the Irish issue of *Seventy3*, in which proved to be the catalyst to producing this book: it was meant as a tribute to Quinn back in November 2011 and coincided with the arrival of Martin O'Neill as manager of Sunderland. Instead it was highlighted how many Irish links we had, so much so, we split the issue in half, offering equal space to both sides of the border in Ireland. Niall was mentioned in parts, but as O'Neill arrived the euphoria of the moment accidently overtook the initial idea of praising Quinn.

The feeling of guilt held by me then was somewhat atoned then when I received an email from one of the writing team informing me that Niall was spotted with the Irish issue on a Ryannair flight. Not one to be a sceptic, I wanted to dispel any outlandish myths before they began and got out of hand – you know the type that frequently accompany the football transfer window – the "Paul Scholes was spotted in Morrison's café" circa 1999 was a particular favourite of mine and the source of the incident would need to be revealed before being used in a public house conversation.

It was loosely confirmed to be true, when the response came that the "spotter" was in fact a friend's mother and had no inkling about football, she just recognised the "tall Irish guy who has something to do with Sunderland" as Quinn and that was good enough for me, Niall Quinn was reading our work, what a moment.

From there the following issue was dubbed a "manager's special" with former Scouse gaffer and the instigator of Quinn's relationship and then love affair with Sunderland, Peter Reid being the guest editor. On interviewing Reid, another writer spoke of why Reidy accepted our offer to be in the magazine. Apparently Reid asked Quinn about our credentials before committing to appear in print, of which Niall apparently replied "it's not an official magazine for the club, but they seem good lads" or something towards that effect. Again loosely confirmed and probably we will never know unless Niall confirms it, this sheer tedious association with the big man, no matter how small or straw clutching, the connection with a real legend in my eyes, was good enough for me and I was on cloud nine.

I was then personally gutted to be present at the recent North-east Derby (October 2012) stood in the hospitality suites aloft in the West Stand of the Stadium of Light, too nervous to eat any food at the thought of what drama could unfold on the pitch that day, chatting away to like minded people also poking at their food with the look of dread on their faces, yet met with a sparkle in the eye, only the bizarre collection of emotions the region's top game can produce, then looking up to see on the TV, this legend, this saviour of Sunderland, the reason we were all here today still enjoying top flight football, chewing on a fine rack of lamb like it was gristle, such was the nerves that day, sat in a studio in the corner of Loftus Road, home of Queen's Park Rangers, sat alongside fellow pundit Ray Wilkins previewing both their game which would take place later that Sunday, but also from afar offering his thoughts on Sunderland versus Newcastle, describing Sunderland as "they" and not "we". This was after all Niall Quinn in the Sky Sports studio sat next to Wilkins.

My heart skipped a beat. Not because of that day's huge game, or probably the extra drop of red wine one has to forcefully endure at these encounters to "get through" the on pitch offerings. No, my heart skipped a beat, when it hit me like a speed train, just how the hell did Niall Quinn end up 350 miles away from Sunderland on a day like today?

I took it personally. He was talking about Sunderland in the impersonal third person persona, as if we were any other football club playing that day, not one where he had rejuvenated his career, or played in goal for, despite being a goal scorer not shot stopper. To use "they" and "them" towards Sunderland when it should have been "we" and "us" so often heard at Niall Quinn's motivational speeches and ad hoc talk-in nights with supporters back in 2006, to get them reinvigorated with the club once more, following a heartbreaking relegation, the season before, well he could have even been talking about other former clubs Arsenal and Manchester City, with whom he had great times, but nothing on the scale of his time on Wearside.

This book project was already underway by the time this incident of note occurred, however once the match was over and bragging rights were shared and divvyed up, *"Magic Carpet Ride"* was out again for the final furlong in full force. This is a tribute book to Niall first and foremost (we also analyse mistakes on the way, as Niall himself has alluded to, I suppose we are all human) the original reason being to simply look back, acknowledge and indeed celebrate what the big man has done for the club, my club. Yet for me, this concept was then overtaken by the desire to prove to Niall Quinn that what he has done for Sunderland AFC over the years has and won't ever be forgotten.

It is a book not about charting how Niall has come to sit in a studio in London doing TV work, rather than be at an important, probably the most important home game of the season for Sunderland and a fixture in which he has history and form. These reasons may unfold in the future, but it is not for us and not our style to prod and provoke and interrogate the reasons why, if there are in fact any at all.

It is a book to highlight the ups and downs; the story of how Niall Quinn paid around £8,000 to drive home stranded Sunderland fans in taxicabs from Bristol, whilst holding it together behind the scenes when your manager is labelling (and some would say quite rightly so) FIFA Vice President, Jack Warner, a clown! Not only that though, it is a book to say, Niall, you are probably the most important man in Sunderland AFC's, the City and surrounding area's modern history. We do not care what may have happened since you have left, but you will always have a place in our hearts for what you have achieved both on and off the pitch, football and non-football related work for the region. Stop calling Sunderland "they" and replace it with "we" and come back once in a while for a drink, hold your head up high, embrace the back slaps and praise and cherish the good times of what you once called a Magic Carpet Ride.

Mal Robinson.
Project Editor, Magic Carpet Ride.
Editor in Chief, *Seventy3* Magazine.

Kevin Phillips Foreword

I signed for Sunderland in the summer of 1997, a lad from down south, whom had only visited the North East before playing for Watford at Roker Park a few years earlier. Little did I know then that I would go on to enjoy the period of success for both me personally and for the club as a whole.

There were many figures at Sunderland, which made this success become a reality. The manager Peter Reid was of course instrumental in it all and gave us the freedom to play. Bobby Saxton as his assistant with his knowledge of the game and wisdom in life. The playing staff who gelled as a unit on and off the pitch, producing a team spirit and bond second to none in my time in the game.

There is though one person that also deserves a special mention and that was my main striker partner at Sunderland – Niall Quinn. When I arrived at the club, Niall had been injured and by his own standards he would admit he had not displayed his best performance to the fans as yet. This would soon change and with two attacking wingers in the form of Allan Johnston and Nicky Summerbee firing in the ammunition for Niall the target man for me to feed off his sublime lay offs and flicks on, we scored a hat full between us that season and for the remaining five years we had together on the pitch.

My relationship and partnership with Quinny was never worked on – it just happened. We just gelled and it took off. Niall was coming back from injury and perhaps at the end of his career, but he was such an intelligent footballer and I fed off that. We never practiced drills or anything. Quinny's role was to be the focal point for defenders and I did the running off him – it worked a treat.

Niall though also had a superb touch for a big man. There have been some standout memories in his playing days on Wearside. The chip against Port Vale, going in goal away to Bradford City and his winner against Newcastle in 2000. He even got away with giving a penalty away in that game, bringing down Robert Lee only for Alan Shearer to miss the resulting spot kick! And of course who could forget his testimonial game, setting a precedent in donating all the proceeds to charities in Sunderland and Dublin?

If all of the above were not enough to cement his place into Sunderland folklore then what he did next and his actions in his second spell at the club must surely have him as God like status up in the North East.

To come back and save a struggling club in 2006 stepping in as temporary manager, Chairman and probably cleaner too knowing Quinny, persuading Roy Keane to come as manager, negotiating new players into the club including the likes of Dwight Yorke in his first season was immense.

Then the stuff of legend, like paying for fan's taxis home at an away game and overcoming the Irish economy crash and having the foresight to appoint Ellis Short means Sunderland have now enjoyed at the time of writing their Seventh consecutive year back in the top flight – something not done since the days Niall was at Sunderland as a player. This will be the legacy in terms of factual evidence, but Niall's legacy to Sunderland overall, both in terms of passion, achievement on and off the pitch and foundations for the future, probably cannot be measured in full.

A Niall Quinn tribute book then in the form of "*Magic Carpet Ride*" is the least the big man deserves and I am delighted to be able to put my name to it.

Best Wishes,

Kevin Phillips
Sunderland AFC 1997–2003.

Niall Quinn Timeline

August 1996 – Signed for Sunderland by manager, Peter Reid for £1.3m.

May 1997 – Suffers relegation with Sunderland from the Premier League after a season out with injury.

May 1998 – Appears and scores a goal in the Play-off final against Charlton Atheltic, which finished 4–4, Sunderland losing 7–6 on penalties. The match was voted one of Wembley's all time greatest games.

May 1999 – Promoted to the Premier League with Sunderland as the club reach a then record of 105 points as Champions.

January 2002 – Announces his testimonial granted by the FAI, with the proceeds going to charity.

May 2002 – Raises over a million pounds for charity from his benefit game at the Stadium of Light, where Sunderland played the Republic of Ireland.

June 2002 – Wins the last of his 92 Republic of Ireland caps at the World Cup in Japan and South Korea.

October 2002 – Plays his last game of football for Sunderland against West Ham United.

November 2002 – Confirms his retirement from football at the age of 35.

July 2006 – Forms and heads the Drumaville consortium, taking control of Sunderland AFC and becomes Chairman of the club.

August 2006 – With no manager at the club, he starts the season as Sunderland manager, before fellow Irishman, Roy Keane is appointed.

March 2007 – Quinn pays for a fleet of taxi cabs for stranded Sunderland fans at an away game against Cardiff City.

May 2007 – Sunderland win the Championship under Keane and are promoted to the Premier League, where they remain to this day.

September 2008 – Texan Billionaire, Ellis Short buys 30% of the Drumaville shares.

December 2008 – Roy Keane resigns as Sunderland manager.

December 2008 – Quinn appoints Ricky Sbragia as manager.

May 2009 – Ricky Sbragia resigns as Sunderland manager.

May 2009 – Ellis Short becomes the sole owner of Sunderland, with Quinn remaining as Chairman.

June 2009 – Quinn appoints Steve Bruce as the next Sunderland manager.

October 2011 – Quinn steps down as Chairman and becomes "Director of International Development".

November 2011 – Steve Bruce is sacked by new Chairman, Ellis Short.

December 2011 – Quinn plays a role in securing Martin O' Neill as new Sunderland manager.

February 2012 – Niall Quinn leaves Sunderland after six years at boardroom level with the club.

Chapter One
Indian Summer

Mal Robinson

When a lanky Irishman arrived at a balmy Roker Park in the summer of 1996, little did anyone think that this new signing for Sunderland would go onto forge a sixteen year football love affair, not matched in the modern game.

Niall John Quinn was signed for Sunderland by then manager – Peter Reid and was hailed as the signing to help keep Sunderland in the Premier League, having themselves only been promoted the previous May. Quinn arrived from Manchester City for a fee of £1.3m having began his career at Arsenal, before moving onto Maine Road, home of Manchester City. The Republic of Ireland international came with high credentials then, as well as the knowledge that a serious cruciate knee ligament injury had hampered his time in the North West with City, however Reid was willing to take a gamble on the front man and after a slow start to life in the North East, the money outlayed by Reid, surely became the shrewdest piece of business in Sunderland's recent history.

Given the shirt number of 17, Quinn soon began to repay some of the money splashed out by Sunderland, starring in a superb 4–1 away win at Nottingham Forest, scoring two goals for his side. This was followed up by another goal in the League Cup at Vicarage Road, Watford, before the cruciate ligament injury flared up once more, in a home game with Coventry City at the back end of September 1996. This was to be Quinn's final involvement of the season, until coming on as a substitute for fellow forward, Paul Stewart in the Lads' then credible away draw with arch rivals – Newcastle United on the fifth of April 1997 and with five games remaining, Sunderland now battling relegation.

Quinn, given the amount of time he had been out was still somewhat short of match practice, sitting in the stands as he watched the promising

Sunderland start to the Premiership campaign, sitting pretty in eleventh place in the league table come the end of January, whittle away to sixteenth in the table on his return to action. He was used on and off the bench in the remainder of the games (including the final home competitive game at Roker Park against Everton) as Sunderland's gradual slide to relegation was confirmed on the last day of the season, Wimbledon sealing the Wearsiders' demise with a Jason Euell goal at Selhurst Park.

The Sunderland fans had not seen anywhere near the best of Niall Quinn, an indifferent beginning then it has to be said to the Irishman's start in the red and white cloth. Something that would repeat itself some ten years later on his return as Sunderland manager.

Things though were about to change.

The summer of 1997 saw the club purchase an array of players to freshen up the place, along with it's much anticipated move from Roker Park to the Sunderland Stadium of Light (SOL). One of those players was a dinky striker named Kevin Phillips, signed from Watford, in a deal many folk in the region were not too excited about. The fans wanted a big name to star up front, although the names soon on everyone's lips was that of Quinn and Phillips, the little man, big man combo, proving to be lethal, as Sunderland, after a hesitant start, began to click into gear. The other new team members including the likes of Jody Craddock and Lee Clark, starting to gel.

It was Quinn himself who made Sunderland history, scoring the first ever goal at the SOL, ironically against his former side – Manchester City, the gangly forward taking advantage of a mislaid back pass, to slot home, the big man almost forgetting who to celebrate in front of, the combination of City fans behind the goal and the new layout of the SOL, thwarting the forward's celebrations seeing the Irishman run towards the away following, before realising his error, eventually celebrating with the sea of red and white.

There were teething problems, with several new players adapting to each other, the growing pressure on the club to bounce back to the Premier League at the earliest opportunity, the opening of the new ground only fuelling this expectation and for Quinn, there was the question hanging over his head, whether he could still perform at this level, following the previous season's plight on the sidelines through injury.

Norwich City at home was most definitely the turning point for both club and Quinn, the hosts losing by a solitary goal, coming after a run of inept performances and defeats, meant the crowd were on everyone's backs, as the tension rose. "Quinny got booed off once when he had knee ligament problems and considered quitting the game, but the lad was brave and turned it around and I cannot talk highly enough of him", added then Sunderland manager, Peter Reid, when talking to *Seventy3* Magazine.

And turn it around he did, as Quinn and Sunderland shot up the table, lighting up the league with a charismatic entertaining style, that had everyone else sitting up taking notice. The combination of the new ground with its stunning facilities and atmosphere and Sunderland's attacking style of play meant attendance's were surpassing 40,000 quite a feat for a Championship standard side, even a midweek game with Reading would churn out a gate of 40,579, the sleeping Sunderland giant had awoken and for Quinn, the Indian summer had begun.

Sunderland's form and on field displays were breathtaking often tearing sides apart. Quinn and Phillips also matched throughout the team with similar partnerships clicking together, such as left back Michael Gray and left winger Allan Johnston, right back Chris Makin and right winger Nicky Summerbee, not to mention the new central defending partnership of Jody Craddock and Darren Williams. Which all meant as a unit Sunderland were often unplayable, the team spirit on many occasions unbreakable, thanks to the frequent team bonding sessions on and away from the training ground.

This was the season Niall Quinn really came into his own, scoring a host of magical goals, including a exquisite chip from just inside the half way line at home to Port Vale, the Irishman already reeling away to celebrate even before the ball had hit the back of the net, such was the confidence about the man and the place in general.

The nervy start to the season though would cost Sunderland dear, the form of eventual champions Nottingham Forest and big spenders down the road at Middlesbrough (eventual runners up) doing enough to secure their automatic promotion places, meaning that with 90 points on the board,

Sunderland were confined to the lottery of the play-offs. Quinn and Sunderland overcame Sheffield United over two legs (the return home leg still talked about today for the blistering speed and atmosphere of the game) to earn a Wembley showdown with Charlton Athletic.

After a shaky start and 1–0 down at half-time, Quinn sent the travelling Mackem masses into delirium leveling the game at 1–1, before pandemonium struck, end-to-end football and pressurised mistakes meaning the contest finished 4–4. After extra time, in what has been voted one of Wembley's greatest games, the Lads' lost out 7–6 on penalties. Local lad Micky Gray missing his spot kick in what turned out to be a blessing in disguise, as Sunderland regrouped and came back stronger the season after.

Niall Quinn later confessed in the following season's club video, how the team grew stronger through that Wembley day's experience, substitute on the day and another local boy – Richard Ord – kicking off team bonding proceedings on the journey home from Wembley, ensuring that following season Sunderland would not require such means to gain promotion, they vowed to achieve the target of promotion no matter what.

And so with the addition of one or two more solid buys, including new centre half, Paul Butler, Sunderland stormed the league, amassing a record 105 points on the way to the title, only suffering their first defeat in November at home to Barnsley, reaching the semi-finals of the League Cup, with the Quinn and Phillips partnership on top form, despite both players suffering injuries throughout the campaign.

Indeed, Quinn played his part at either end of the team in a matter of weeks, as winter made way for spring. The big man popped up in the penalty box to poke in a vital last minute winner at home to Wolves, erupting the SOL into a state of hysteria, whilst only a smattering of games later and Quinn was at it again, heading in the only goal of the game at promotion rivals Bradford City, later volunteering to go into goal to replace the concussed Thomas Sorensen (those were the days of no substitute goalkeeper on the bench) and performing what can only be described as a "Superman" save near the end of the match, as Quinny flew through the air, in the same grace and style of the super hero from Krypton, albeit missing the ball by a mile, ensuring this goalkeeping moment has been written into Wearside cult status for its comical elements. Quinn saw the funny side at the time, yet on a serious note, he enabled Sunderland to a clean sheet and an important step to promotion.

Quinn was on hand again to help Sunderland to a 4–1 half time lead away at Gigg Lane, Bury – a game that saw them clinch automatic promotion, the result finishing in a 5–2 away win, the Quinn (one goal) and Phillips (four goals) combination proving too hot to handle once more…cue the celebrations. Days later the job was done and the lads were crowned Champions away at Barnsley, still with three games to spare.

"The '99 squad I knew would do it and get the title. Off the back of that Play-off final defeat, the team was destined to go up. The team could have gone the other way and collapsed and the Wembley defeat was no one's fault, the issue was a few games before when we lost a two goal lead at home to QPR around Easter time. We were a bit naïve and a young side, but a very good side. Quinn and Phillips were top drawer and come the summer after that disappointment we all knew promotion would finally happen, so actually the whole squad just expected to win every week and this showed with the 105 points tally" reflects then Sunderland boss, Peter Reid.

Sunderland's phenomenal form carried over into the following season as virtually the same team that had stormed the Championship, did likewise with the top flight of England. Quinn again was a pivotal figure early on, scoring his first goal of the season in monsoon like conditions away to Sunderland's fierce rivals, Newcastle United, furthermore endearing himself to the legions of Sunderland fans, as strike partner, Kevin Phillips, notched the winner in a fine 2–1 victory, still talked about on Wearside today.

Seventh place was attained that season for Sunderland, with Niall continuing his Indian summer, chipping in with 14 goals, the big man little man partnership with Phillips now feared as much in the Premiership as it was a league lower, Phillips earning himself the Golden Boot for leading goal scorer in Europe, but it was all about the partnership of the veteran Irishman and the up and coming Englishman, a partnership which reflected another Sunderland front duo, some ten years previous, formed by then ageing striker Eric Gates, with young hot shot, Marco Gabbiadini. Back then it was deemed that Gates had helped introduce and bring on Gabbiadini in the game, with his intrinsic football brain and deft touches to create the chances for Marco Goalo as he was known then, whilst Gabbiadini had returned the favour in kind, extending Gates' career by several years, drawing the players to him with a turn of blistering pace, allowing the former Ipswich Town man Gates the time to join his partner on the score sheet. Roll on a decade and Kevin Phillips had seemingly spurred on the evergreen Quinn, doing the big man's running for him, whilst Quinn paid the young starlet back, with clever flicks and lay offs, both reaping the rewards from each other's game, introducing Phillips to the England international stage and Quinn a path towards the 2002 World Cup finals with Ireland, following the pair's progress in that and the next season for Sunderland.

The 2000–01 season reached the standard of the three previous seasons on Wearside for the club and for the strike partnership of Quinn and Phillips. Indeed it was Quinn who got Sunderland off to the perfect start on the opening day, scoring the winner against his old club, Arsenal, in a hard fought 1–0 win, that set the tone for the season.

Niall's fourth goal of the season though would ensure his name was already etched in Sunderland history and the promotion to cult status. After equalising against Newcastle in the North-east Derby at St. James' Park the season before, Quinn went one better this season, heading in the winner, following another free flowing Sunderland counter attack, that had graced the Premier League since 1999. The travelling fans were sent into raptures and even Quinn's luck of the Irish continued for Sunderland, when the gangly forward found himself defending in his own penalty box, eventually conceding a penalty after a illegal challenge on Newcastle's Robert Lee.Saw Alan Shearer's spot kick saved by Sunderland keeper, Thomas Sorensen to spare the big man's blushes!

Come the end of the season, Sunderland finished once more in Seventh place, Quinn having scored eight goals in 37 appearances, yet this tally only tells half the story. Once more his vision and ability to hold the ball up and bring others into play and form an attacking position, meant Quinn was held in high esteem by the Wearside faithful, but his reputation both on and off the pitch was about to explode off the scale come the next campaign.

Sunderland's bid to finish the season again in the top ten of English football took a knock and they only escaped with the skin of their teeth finishing one place above relegation. Even though it was not quite last day drama stuff, Sunderland had witnessed so many times before, it was considered something of a negative season for the club, yet top flight status had been maintained. Niall Quinn was actually Sunderland's top appearance holder for the season with 38 appearances (14 as substitute) in red and white, with six goals in total.

It was not so much Quinn's efforts on the pitch for Sunderland than stood out, although, his work ethic and high standards were of course upheld and enjoyed by fans, but his decision to donate all of his testimonial (granted that season by the Football Association of Ireland for service to his country) proceeds to two charities (one Children's Hospital unit in Dublin and one in Sunderland) that caught the headlines across the world and captured the hearts of the supporters, both in the North East, in Ireland and beyond.

Sunderland Chairman at the time, Sir Bob Murray told the world's press: "Niall Quinn is an eloquent and exceptional person, a statesman in the game. It is an honour for us to host this match on his behalf and to be so well associated with the Irish team before they leave for the World Cup."

Indeed it was to be one of Ireland's final warm up games before departing for the 2002 World Cup in Japan and South Korea, weeks before the infamous Roy Keane walk out of the Irish camp, which would go on to form the basis for Quinn's autobiography, years later, but all forgotten about when Quinn appointed Keane as his first Sunderland manager as Chairman.

Quinn played both halves of the game, most likely embarrassed by all of the attention, one half in Sunderland colours, one in Irish. The embarrassment of it all was evident when explaining his decision in the January of that year to the press. "This game and the money we are going to raise, it isn't me standing up and deserving credit," he told the *Sunday Times*. "This is my way of fighting my demons, my way of saying, `Look I am sorry for giving in to the temptations'. I have abused the privileged life I have had and if this match is anything, it is me paying my debt. I am uncomfortable with the way football is going, has gone. If I hadn't become a professional footballer, if I had stayed in Ireland and got a job, I think I would have been a far better person. I am convinced of that. That's the debt and it's something that crosses my mind every week."

Quinn even appeared on the BBC's "*Breakfast with Frost*" in March, 2002, following a defeat to Chelsea the day before, stating again the reasons and explanation on the behind the scenes work to get the match to go ahead, thanks to the efforts of Sunderland Chairman, Murray.

"Well I kind of made my mind up many years ago, the feeling was that if I ever was lucky enough to reach the quota that it would be a nice payback thing to do. Because I mean I'm still living the life of the dream, you know, the schoolboy dream that I always had - I'm 35 years of age, still living it, and of course I'm paid very well to boot so I just felt if I ever reached the quota of caps for Ireland, which was 50 originally, that I would give the game to charity. Obviously that was over a period of time, I reached 49 caps and the goalposts were moved, they were moved from 50 to 75, so I thought it wasn't going to work out but then I got to 74 and it was also capped - sorry the caps were stopped completely and so the testimonials were finished. So I just missed out and I made the point to my chairman one day, Bob Murray at the races – my Sunderland chairman – that if only they'd known that I was going to give the game to charity maybe they'd have allowed me have it, and somewhere along the way he thought I'll try and put that in place and fantastically he came up with the goods and the mechanism was in place for me to stage the game at the Stadium of Light, which would have a bigger crowd and a more meaningful game than perhaps, you know, a smaller game in Dublin on a rented pitch."

A crowd of 35,702 attended the benefit game on 14 of May 2002, dubbed by the club as "A night with Niall". However it was the brainwave of non-attendance tickets sold to fans across the globe as a souvenir of the night, ideal for people who could not make the game, yet still show their support for the good cause, meant the target of a million pounds was reached.

The season after following a decent show by Quinn and the Republic of Ireland at that summer's World Cup, despite the scandal of Roy Keane's sudden departure, was a disaster for Sunderland, whilst personally for Quinn, it signaled the end of his 19 year football career.

Peter Reid, the man who had brought Quinn to Sunderland to enjoy his Indian summer, was sacked in October 2002, following a poor start to the season. A start which saw Quinn fail to make the first eleven in any of Sunderland's games due to a persistent back injury, that would eventually force his retirement from the game, which he announced publicly in November of 2002, following his last appearance for Sunderland against West Ham United at home on 19 October.

The game against West Ham was Howard Wilkinson's first game in charge of Sunderland, following Reid's dismissal, with Quinn named on the substitute's bench, coming on for fellow striker Marcus Stewart on the hour mark. Football is a game filled with quirky facts and acts of fate, that tend to come around in circles and whilst Quinn was pulling on the red and white jersey for the final time, future Sunderland manager, Paolo Di Canio set up West Ham's winner that day, the Londoners ensuring Quinn bowed out with a 0–1 home defeat, despite the Irishman's best efforts, Niall hitting the post towards the end of the game.

Unbeknown to Quinn that day, would be the fact that he would have a indirect hand in Di Canio becoming Sunderland's twenty-ninth full time manager. Years later the newly retired striker would invite Texan billionaire, Ellis Short to become Sunderland Chairman, who would then go on to appoint Di Canio as Sunderland "Head Coach".

Quinn was offered an immediate coaching role by then Sunderland boss, Wilkinson, however the former striker turned this down, as he explained to BBC Sport. "I turned it down – not out of disrespect but because I don't think I really want to be a football coach. Peter Reid was the only person I would have been a coach for before and as he got the sack 12 weeks later I don't think I did a very good job. I am just going to spend a couple of months thinking about my future."

The glow on Niall Quinn's Indian summer had simmered; the light now burning out, the boots hung up for good. For Sunderland, the same could be said that season, the renaissance of the Reid years now starting to disintegrate after his sacking earlier that season, Howard Wilkinson's tenure at the SOL lasted a mere 27 games, with 15 losses – many heavy.

Again another quirky Quinn football link, meant that his former International boss, Mick McCarthy was charged with keeping the club afloat late into the season, being the club's third manager in one campaign, but by then the rot had set it and Sunderland were relegated with a then record low of 19 points. Despite McCarthy leading Sunderland to two semi-finals the following season (FA Cup semi-final against Millwall (lost 0–1) and the Play-off semi final against Crystal Palace (lost on penalties) Sunderland failed to clinch promotion. This was attained the season after under McCarthy and whilst the success was commendable, a certain degree of damage had been inflicted on the club, following such an embarrassing relegation in 2003. If fans with skeptical views were still angry at the club's poor showing that season, then worse was to come.

In the top flight campaign of 2005–06 it quickly became clear that McCarthy's cheaply assembled team was no match for the Premier League, only managing one home win all season, McCarthy was relieved of his duties and made way for former fan favourite and then Assistant Academy coach – Kevin Ball to act as Caretaker Manager. Ball's task though was too much to ask and whilst performances improved, it was too little too late for Sunderland, the side somehow eclipsing their 19 point total in 2003, with an abysmal 15 point showing, breaking their own all time low record in the process.

The club was wounded, hemorrhaging players who wanted away, the summer of 2006 proved to be a long one, with the outlook of a possible double relegation down to League 1, not entirely out of the equation, such was the gloom surrounding Wearside, as the fans looked on with woe.

Yet on 3 of July 2006, after much speculation a take over was on the cards, back came fan's favourite Niall Quinn to head an Irish consortium of businessmen, named the Drumaville consortium, of which Niall fronted and took over as Chairman of Sunderland, in a bid to rebuild the club and do their upmost to repeat the Indian Summer, Quinn had enjoyed as a player in front of the Sunderland masses.

In 2006 though, the hypothetical sun cream was abandoned and seat-belts were locked in, as Niall's Indian summer was swapped for the "Magic Carpet Ride", he promised the fans on his return as head of Sunderland's boardroom, in a speech to the public outside the front doors of the SOL.

Sunderland and its fans, never let down by Quinn on the pitch, were not going to be let down with his promise of a rollercoaster journey of emotion. The Indian summer had finished; Quinn's Sunderland sojourn had begun.

Chapter Two
Quinn's Return

Chris O'Hara

2006 was a tempestuous year for Sunderland AFC. Following a humiliating relegation from the Premier League, their second such trauma in the space of four years, the club was at a real crossroads. Crowds were dwindling and the prospect of another season in the Championship was not appealing. Having seen the team manage a measly 19 and 15 points in their previous attempts, it was becoming abundantly clear that in Sunderland, we did not have a team capable of sitting comfortably at the top table of the Premier League.

The chairman at the time, Bob Murray was no longer capable of bankrolling the team to the extent required to establish themselves in the Premier League and rumours doing the rounds suggested he had almost bankrupted the club moving into the Stadium of Light. Dark days lay ahead, with no apparent light at the end of the tunnel. This was a traumatic time for a club once labelled 'The Bank of England Club' in the early 1950's. A club with a glorious history, having won the league six times in the past and of course the famous FA Cup victories, was in serious danger of dropping into oblivion with a white elephant of a stadium.

So with no manager, relegation confirmed, a largely empty stadium and a skint chairman, Sunderland AFC was not quite a sleeping giant, more a giant on life support, waiting for the plug to be pulled to put it out of its misery.

While the North East was not exactly flush and full of the joys of spring the Irish economy was in overdrive. Buoyed by the Celtic Tiger, the Republic of Ireland was enjoying a boom of industry, technology and growth, the likes of which had never been seen before. For a country more used to famine and fighting, one man never forgot his roots.

Yes he may have been born in Perrystown and learned his trade at Arsenal and Manchester City but Niall Quinn has never made a secret of his love for Sunderland. Rarely does a team get under the skin of a player but Quinn embraced the area, the fans and the history of this once great side. Always hailed as a legend while donning the famous red and white stripes, he had given the current crop of supporters some of their greatest moments at the Stadium of Light. He would forever be the man who scored the first goal, netting the first in a 3–1 win over former employers Manchester City at the Stadium.

Footballers make a very good living from the clubs that employ them but some players are just different. Playing for the love of the game and the fans, understanding what it means to be adored and using that to better yourself as a person rather than your bank balance. Niall Quinn is such a man having famously donated his testimonial fee to children's charities in 2002.

In truth, the thought of a new leadership at Sunderland was mooted long before the eventual takeover. In March of 2006, *BBC News* reported that Quinn was interested in taking over the reins on Wearside, a claim dismissed by the club at the time. Although at this point Murray did advise that he was willing to relinquish his stake in the club.

By mid-April though the bid was coming together as Quinn gathered together his mysterious band of Irish businessmen ready to rescue the club he loved. Quoted in the *Irish Independent* he did reveal that the bid was far from finished. Obviously acutely aware that any bid put forward would be subject to intense scrutiny from not only the board at the club but also the press and supporters throughout the world, Quinn admitted:

"It is not about putting money on the table and making an offer for a football club. We have to prove to ourselves before we go near any fans or any club, we are capable of running a football club. It is a jungle, as I have found out in the last three weeks. It is not a simple thing at all and that is what I am in the middle of – making sure myself and my group are capable of doing a job this club deserves. Until we get to the bottom of that we cannot possibly approach Sunderland. We want to be ready for Sunderland so every question they ask we can answer them dynamically about what is going to happen."

While proving that he had an astute business head in not showing his full deck of cards, Quinn also revealed his other reasons for wanting to take over the club. A quote that he would use to full effect in the pubs and clubs of the North East later down the line was first coined as follows:

"I am afraid of nothing at that football club. When I was up there it was like being on a magic carpet when things were going well. The emotion of the people when they are in good form and the club is going well is something to behold. Newcastle get 53,000 and they are a pretty big club. Everybody thinks they are far bigger than Sunderland but I know if this club goes right we will be bigger than Newcastle. That is what attaches me to it. It is the potential, it is the people, it is their spirit."

So while Quinn was clearly the face of the takeover, what of the other so far anonymous businessmen looking to invest in a club from the Emerald Isle? The Drumaville Consortium charged with the takeover bid consisted of eight men, mostly property developers and all previously associated with Quinn in other ventures, restricted to Ireland.

The main man behind the takeover and major shareholder in the apparently secretive consortium turned out to be Paddy Kelly. Paddy took on 2,360 shares in the consortium and can rightly lay claim to being the money next to Quinn's popularity power. A property developer by trade, Kelly owns Kelland Homes, Rockbriar and Markland holdings. With an estimated wealth of £80 million he was certainly the wealthiest shareholder.

Not far behind in the relative terms of millionaire-dom is Louis Fitzgerald. The 2006 Rich List showing that he had amassed a not inconsiderable £59 million through the more traditional Irish pastime of drinking. Owning a wide selection of pubs and clubs throughout Dublin, Fitzgerald is well known for his licenced property portfolio. Ranked ninety-sixth in Irelands richest men (only 86 places behind Bono) he took on 1,180 shares in the club.

Also taking on 1,180 shares in the club were Jack Tierney, John Hays and Patsy Byrne. Tierney and Byrne are again both property developers, making their connections with Quinn throughout his various building projects. Respectively, Tierney owns and operates Faxhill homes while Byrne is one half of Byrne Bros, one of the UK's leading concrete frame contractors.

John Hays still retains a place on the board after the Irish connection has now departed and has been vice chairman of the club. He is the only member of Drumaville to be Sunderland born and bred. Owner of Hays Travel, a well-known and successful travel agency based in the North East, he provided a valuable ingredient to the consortium of what it means to be a Sunderland supporter. Hays Travel is in fact the largest independent travel agency in the UK and one of The *Sunday Times* Best UK Companies to Work For in the UK.

John's story will strike a chord with many a Sunderland fan and across the region as a whole. Coming from a family of 6, living in a one bed-roomed cottage, John started life as a miner's son. His mother was struck down with rheumatic fever at 30 and was told she would be bedridden for the rest of her life. Speaking to *BQ Magazine*, John Hays continues: "Shortly after my brother Malcolm was born, my mother was very ill. For a couple of years she was in hospital or bedridden.

"My brother, who was five years younger, went as a baby to live with Uncle Tom and Auntie Nancy, who had no children then. Bringing Malcolm home later was traumatic. I remember him crying for his 'mother', who was actually his auntie. I lived with my grandparents in the two-up-two-down.

"Even when I came back, my mam was always in bed downstairs at the front window, seeing what was going on. Rheumatic fever had damaged her heart. She could have said, 'that's it', but at 38, with my dad a pit joiner and no money whatsoever, she borrowed £50 from my grandfather Tom Moffat – a Wearmouth miner - to get a credit facility at Joplings." The Sunderland department store paid her commission to win customers. From this, Hays Credit was founded, still run today by brother Malcolm.

Offered the chance to move to the City and become a merchant banker, John turned down the opportunity, stating he enjoyed the sums but didn't like doing deals.

His beloved mothers love for Sunderland rubbed off on John and she was immensely proud to see him installed as vice-chairman before her passing in 2009. A well respected member of the north-east community, his name on the list of shareholders provided a welcome slice of local flavour to proceedings.

Pat Beirne, our penultimate shareholder and also smallest investor, took on just 738 shares and is managing director of Mergon Ltd.

Saving the best for last, there is of course the one man who captured the imagination of the supporters throughout the takeover process. This of course was the infamous Charlie Chawke, the owner of a chain of pubs in Ireland and best known for being shot in 2003 and robbed of 48000 euros. Also known to be a close friend of Bertie Aherne, the almost Dickensian character was immediately taken to heart by the supporters. Owner of The Bank pub in the heart of Dublin, Chawke was famed for giving free pints of Guinness to anybody entering from Sunderland. Still to be seen regularly in the pub, he is a genial character, never short of a word or two and who was a social investor, rather than a man out to make a profit from the club. In 2009 he was also the subject of cheeky speculation over buying out Mike Ashley at Newcastle United. Although quotes can be attributed to Chawke over this, the legitimacy of his interest is still the subject of speculation amongst Sunderland supporters, thinking he may be using that famed sparkling Irish wit.

"We're looking at it, alright," Chawke said. "It's a great club. He [Ashley] is looking for £100m. You could probably get it for less with a bit of luck. A year-and-a-half ago he was looking for £600m. The problem is to get the syndicate together. Our syndicate in Sunderland bust up last year so a few of us are interested again but others are not, so we will just have to look at trying to get a few people interested in it."

So there we have it. The crew assembled from Eire (and Sunderland) to steer the good ship Sunderland AFC from the murky waters of oblivion and on to Premier League stability and success. Once the interest in the club was confirmed by Quinn, the takeover itself appeared to be a formality. The reputation of Quinn and the promise of investment immediately brought the fans onside. After being fed poor fare for many years, relying on youth and tired legs, this appeared to be a chance to invest in a product on the pitch ready to complement the off field activities.

To give Bob Murray his dues, the man invested heavily in making Sunderland a product and left a fine legacy in the magnificent Stadium of Light and state of the art Academy of Light. The beloved though dilapidated Roker Park was no longer a viable option for an aspiring Premiership side and as much as it was heart wrenching to leave, the move to the banks of the River Wear can hold testament to the fact that Murray had only the best interests of the club at heart.

Although a float on the Stock Exchange was ultimately unsuccessful, Murray always held the future security and reputation of the club at his forefront.

Speaking to the *Northern Echo* in October 2012, Murray says:

"I always wanted us to be an ethical club. We never got in trouble with the FA or got bad headlines."

Bob's expertise in major construction projects and reputation within football led to his appointment to the Wembley board in 2002 to ensure the new national stadium was contracted successfully. In November 2008, the FA appointed him as project director for the National Football centre, St George's Park which opened in late 2012. "What makes me proud of my time with Sunderland? The legacy of the Stadium, the Academy and the concerts hosted there every summer. And we do amazing things at the Foundation of Light like getting grandmas and granddaughters with literacy problems to work together side-by-side. Things like that are so important. I love this region and I want people in the north-east to get a better start in life than I had."

Talk of the takeover was confirmed by Quinn in April 2006 although it was over a week before Murray himself confirmed the club was listening to potential bidders.

Then, silence.

As is always the way in big money, corporate ventures, a period of secrecy and due diligence followed. Although frustrating for supporters keen on seeing big money spent on new players and a new manager, hoping to see a renewed vigour in the club, this was a wait they had to endure. A further two months followed before Murray announced he would be standing down as chairman as of the 30 June 2006.

"I have done this job for 20 years and I know for a fact that 99% of the fans are good humoured and want the best for the club," Murray told the *Sunderland Echo*. "I do, too, and if it means I need to resign to make the sale happen, then that is what I will do. I want fans to know for certain that I will not be the chairman of this football club at the start of next season.

"I have never been upset by personal comments, but some people are. I've given so much to this club over the years, but it's time for me to take a back seat. I don't want personalities to be an issue."

With that, the seeds were sewn for Quinn and the Drumaville Consortium to step up and take control. So it came to pass that on 3 of July 2006, Sunderland AFC made the announcement eagerly awaited by fans around the globe. That a bid had been accepted and Niall Quinn would be installed as chairman. The takeover itself valued the club at around £10 million. Although some may say £9.9 million of this was the property portfolio, at last the club was in new hands. As of 27 July 2006 Drumaville Ltd took full control of Sunderland, with possession of 89.13% of shares in Sunderland Ltd.

Quinn said: "My consortium are buying into the wonderful potential at the club and wish to help enable it to regain the status it truly deserves. I am personally delighted on behalf of my company Drumaville to be in position to present this offer to the shareholders of Sunderland. We believe this heralds a new beginning for Sunderland, but it's only going to happen if everyone comes together in a joint effort. "Over the last few weeks, I've made it quite plain that I believe it's one of the greatest football clubs in the world that is in fantastic shape everywhere but on the pitch.

"I hope that by being a former player here, by knowing what makes things tick at Sunderland, that I will add something intriguing and new that a chairman perhaps hasn't been in a position to do before here, all based with an emphasis to getting it right on the pitch. I can't thank the people involved enough for allowing this to happen, especially Bob Murray, who agreed with me it was time for a difference to be made and paved the way for me to do that. I really want to knit everybody back together again so the people of Sunderland will see what this club is all about, they will see the passion again and the football team can be reunited to the fans. That's the biggest message I want to give about my term here. I know what it's like when these fans are behind the team and the team plays to it's maximum potential. I really firmly believe if I can reconnect the players to the people and the club in general to the people, and the passion flows around the stadium with its positive charges, this team will get back to where it deserves to be."

With control of the club now established, Quinn faced an uphill battle on three fronts. Fans had become disillusioned with the club. A severe lack on investment in the team, multiple relegations and poor footballing fare had seen a drop in attendances. Allied to the fact that the team had no manager and a poor crop of recently relegated players, his work was certainly cut out.

Quinns first port of call was to get back on side with the fans. Football chairman are by and large an elusive species. Hiding in the boardroom, avoiding confrontation with fans, signing cheques and trying to keep their heads below the parapet. Quinn was different. Here was a man who knew the passion and pride of Wearside. He knew the fans were pining for better times but after so many false dawns and failures, it was all a bit much to believe that the glory days were here again. In an unprecedented step, Quinn took the decision to go back to the streets, engage the fans and allay fears. His plan was to visit local pubs, clubs and bars. The hotbeds of Sunderland, Wearside and County Durham were targeted by Quinn as he looked to rein-vigorate the passion and pride he had experienced in the halcyon days of Peter Reid. Don't be mistaken, this wasn't a begging mission by any means. Quinn was not only out to ensure he presented an attractive opportunity, he was also there to call out to so called 'armchair supporters' and ask them why they had lost the faith and what it would take to bring them back. Speaking at the Rainton Meadows Arena in front of around 500 sceptical and hopeful fans Quinn said, "Be tough on me, because I'm going to be tough on you, The potential at this football club is absolutely enormous but we can't say we're a big football club with 23,000 people in the ground. I understand the economic climate and I understand that jobs are being lost, but all I would ask is that you do everything you can to support us. We can't do any of this without you."

He continued the empassioned plea: "I know you've been let down in the past, I'm not going to promise anything in terms of what we might achieve, but I can promise you how we are going to go about it. We are barely £1m in debt in terms of the transfer fees we have paid since taking over the club, and the long-term debt will be paid in ten years. My people at Drumaville are not football people, they're sporting people, and they want to see this club get a sporting chance."

This theme continued up and down the region and ensured the legend that was Niall Quinn 'Our Chairman' will be forever remembered amongst the fans.

Stage two and three of Quinn's rebuilding of the club involved the tricky matter of the footballing aspect of the club. All is well and good filling a stadium with expectant fans but there needs to be more on the pitch than white lines and goalposts. Having seen the team relegated with a record low tally not three months earlier, time was becoming tight to appoint a manager and invest in the team in preparation for the long season ahead in the Championship. Being relegated once is not the ideal scenario when taking charge of a club but another season of struggle and potential relegation is an idea not worth contemplating.

Quinn was looking for the inspirational man to take the reins. That manager who inspired confidence and attracted the players who would look to fire the team back to the pinnacle of English football. Having seen his attempts thwarted to sign Martin O'Neill (the first time around) and also Sam Allardyce, Quinn was finding his options limited. With pre-season already in full swing and the season a matter of days away, the onus once again fell on St Niall to rescue his beloved club.

He said: "When I was in full flow with the club three months ago, becoming manager is not something I thought I would be doing. But it has transpired that way, even though the group who are backing me could not have been more ambitious in trying to attract a world-class manager. What happened is that we decided we would try to attempt the first hurdle because what we have to do is try to stop the slide, to turn the corner. We have to gather momentum, and then to lift it so that we get to a point where I can pick the phone up, go to a world-class manager and hopefully with the position we are then in, say to him 'come now'."

Quinns first day in the job could not have been more difficult. Having dealt with the fans and made promises of better times around the corner, the failure to attract a manager also hit closer to home. Faced with a team of players looking to abandon ship, Quinn faced a mammoth task.

Taking over the story, speaking to the *Journal*, Quinn continues: "I ended up at the training ground on my first day with 24 professional footballers who had been relegated on a low points tally the season before. I had to do something about it, it was seven days to the first game. I then thought I was a manager – which was my first mistake! I decided I would see the players one by one and do it alphabetically. The first player who came to see me was goalkeeper Ben Alnwick. He handed me a transfer request. I was a little bit disappointed, as you can imagine. I thought very quickly, 'You only have two goalkeepers, you had better go and get the other one.' Kelvin (Davies) was the other one and I wanted to make sure he was OK, so I asked him how he was. He said, 'I am fine', then handed me a transfer request. I sent him to get Ben back in and told him, 'Ben, you have a new three-year contract, you are playing on Saturday. Do you want your transfer request back?' He took it back. I was so pleased because the next name was Julio Arca, who I played with for six years. He walked in and said, 'Quinny! I must go'. Things were tough, so I turned to the man I had brought in to help me, (assistant manager) Bobby Saxton. He walked into the players' communal area and the whole place went silent. He said, 'Right you lot, there is a rumour going around one or two of you want to stay at this club. Is that right?' There was silence. So I carried on down the list and everyone of them came in and said they were happy at the club."

So the inaugural game came about and a trip to the Ricoh Arena to face Coventry was first up for the Championships newest boys. Sunderland fans have not always shared a loving relationship with Coventry City due another chairman's antics. Famously Jimmy Hill was integral in seeing the kick-off of Coventry's final game of the season delayed by ten minutes so he would know the final result and therefore what result Coventry would need to avoid relegation. A fact that still sticks in the craw of many a red and white supporter. Nevertheless, Coventry it was and Niall Quinn was about to make his debut as Sunderland Chairman/Manager, surely a first for the club, and based on experience, hopefully a last. Featuring a strong Irish contingent, Sunderland took to the field, hopefully ready to start a new era of success and joy. Kenny Cunningham, Rory Delap, Liam Lawrence, Stephen Elliott and Daryl Murphy forming the Irish spine of the team with experience, skill and pace. The first half was largely forgettable on a hot day in August. Sunderland fans, happy to be drawing were in dreamland on 52 minutes as Daryl Murphy slotted home to put the away side a goal to the good. Was it too good to be true? Could Niall Quinn, Sunderland saviour and chairman also be Niall Quinn, managerial master? Well, as it turned out, no. Goals from Stern John and Gary McSheffrey saw all three points going into Coventry's win column.

Quinn went on to take charge of another five games, losing four and bringing his managerial career to a close with a 2–0 win over West Bromwich Albion.

While openly admitting that he was not management material, Quinn was struggling to put the final piece of the puzzle together to complete the takeover proper. Who was the man to take charge on the field? Who could provide inspiration to a team sorely lacking in confidence? Who could light up the fans, the stadium, the world? While many names had been mentioned, one was never thought to be on the agenda. Following a huge bust up in 2002 during the World Cup, Niall Quinn and Roy Keane endured a frosty relationship at best. To suggest that this could lead to an employer/employee relationship was unthinkable. However, on 29 August 2006, Roy Keane was unveiled as Sunderland manager. Having met the players shortly before the West Brom game and watching from the stands, Quinn was suitably impressed with what he saw.

"When Roy met players, you could almost see them standing an inch or two taller thinking 'we are going to be working with that man, that is incredible'," added Quinn. Possibly, the players are a bit scared. I hope they are, not in the sense they will under perform but that they will give their all when they go training. This is a very demanding place but standards are going to have to be lifted. You only have to spend a short amount of time in Roy's company to realise just how impressive he is."

During his unveiling Keane of course used the opportunity to give an insight into his thinking and ideas for the rest of the season. "I'm not looking to make too many changes too quickly without seeing what's there first." Harking back to the famous spat, he said, "I've fallen out with thousands of people, but I'm humble enough to apologise if I think I've done something wrong." Finally, when asked about his famed addiction to perfection, supposedly the source of all the 2002 troubles, Keane shot back, "All I ever expected from my teammates was 100%. I spoke to the players this morning and said if they give 100% to Sunderland there won't be a problem. If they take their eye off the ball and don't give 100%, then there will be a problem." A challenge not many people would want to take lightly.

So there we have it, a tale of secretive Irish investors, led by a Sunderland legend and a Sunderland supporter, looking to rescue a club from oblivion. With a fiery young manager in charge and a renewed passion amongst the fans, the pieces of the puzzle were all falling nicely into place. The rest of the tale, from play-offs to promotion, to stability and to the final selling of the club are still to be revealed. For now, SundIreland was a good place to be, only after a run of games with Niall as manager, which set the blood pressure sky high.

Chapter Three
Niall Quinn – The Manager

Gary Emmerson

Six games. 540 minutes. Five defeats. One victory. Arguably the lowest point of recent Sunderland history: an embarrassing cup defeat to bottom of the football league Bury. That is Niall Quinn's brief managerial career in a nutshell and it doesn't add much to his glittering CV.

In his defence, the facts and figures don't tell the entire story of the goings-on at the club at the time. After all, at one moment Quinn, never really management material in the first place, was on the training ground attempting to not only motivate a squad who had just suffered the embarrassment of the 15 point relegation from the Premier League, but also attempting to add bodies, and with it quality, to his squad. Players to whom *Seventy3* magazine have spoken have understandably joked that the only things Quinn was not attempting to do at this time were to drive the team bus and be kit-man.

That can't have been easy for a man who, at the same time, had become Chairman, replacing Bob Murray, following the takeover of the club by the Drumaville Consortium he had been instrumental in putting together. We are familiar with the concept of the player-manager but, with a few madcap exceptions like Ron Noades, the role of Chairman-Manager is a novelty.

He didn't have to do any of it, taking on the managerial role or saving the club from potential financial ruin. After all, he had retired as a player four years earlier. But he had taken Sunderland AFC to his heart, in the same way the fans had taken him to their heart during his six years at the Stadium of Light, and Roker Park for that matter before it, during the glorious swansong to his career, and was not about to sit around and watch his adopted club do what we now know to be a "Leeds".

While finalising the boardroom takeover with the consortium he had personally formed from contacts in his native Ireland, Quinn decided he would play the role of manager too. Who else would have wanted a job at a club where the owners hadn't even signed on the dotted line? Quinn felt he had only one option: to do it himself until things had fallen into place in the boardroom.

Transfer Activity

New faces arriving in pre-season were largely free transfer signings with funding unavailable due to the ongoing takeover talks. Kenny Cunningham, a former Republic of Ireland international team-mate of Quinn's joined as did fellow defender and Magpie Robbie Elliott as well as goalkeeper Darren Ward at no cost to bolster the holes left by the departures of the likes of fans' favourite Julio Arca and very much not fan's favourite goalkeeper Kelvin Davis.

Then, during a miserable start to the season, came the sale of George McCartney to West Ham with Clive Clarke, another known to Quinn from his international days, making the opposite journey as part of the deal. Kevin Kyle, the striker, was offloaded to Coventry City and, presumably in a desperate attempt to add a spark to a squad who had started the campaign in the worst possible way as the hangover left by the relegation from the Premier League continued to thump firmly, Quinn looked overseas as he signed Arnau Riera and William Mocquet. It is fair to say that these last two signings prompted widespread bemusement although such is the talismanic charisma of Spain in general and Barcelona in particular that Wearside pubs witnessed many knowing predictions as to Riera's skill and panache. Not having heard of him before was, of course, not an issue.

Spanish midfielder Riera arrived on Wearside from the Barcelona B team, where he had captained a certain Lionel Messi, prompting optimism that he would be the type of playmaker that was critically needed. But that proved to be a dream of the most elaborate proportions as Riera's Sunderland career was brief, playing 35 minutes as a substitute in a defeat at Southend before being sent off just four minutes into his first start for the club at Bury in the League Cup. Riera was anything but a steal, even as a free transfer signing. Quinn had thought he was getting a talented midfield dynamo, not one who would end up at Falkirk.

Mocquet, signed from French minnows Le Havre, didn't even get on the pitch for four minutes during two years at the Stadium of Light. Whatever the potential possessed by the right-winger was, unsuccessful loans spells at Rochdale and Bury clearly underlined him as one of Quinn's failures in the transfer market as a manager. Still you can't really blame the guy; his head must have been spinning; performing roles on the training ground, in the transfer market, with the press and media and in the boardroom, all while sorting out the intricate workings of his consortium too.

One deal, perhaps, he did get right was Tobias Hysen, the son of the former Liverpool defender Glenn who joined in a £1.7 million deal prior to Quinn's final game, and only win, in the dugout. Hysen played plenty of key roles in the 2006–07 season, most notably on his debut when lighting up a literally half-empty Stadium of Light, a spark much needed at the time, which sadly was his only year on Wearside.

Pre-Season

Bobby Saxton, Peter Reid's former sidekick in the home dressing room at both Roker Park and the Stadium of Light, agreed to return briefly to help out Quinn following a "phone a friend" type phone call. It was expertise that Quinn needed, not the answer to a million pound question. The answer from Saxton was yes and he was joined in the dugout during four pre-season friendlies by Kevin Richardson. In a curtailed pre-season programme, largely down to the ongoing off-field behind-the-scenes discussions and takeover talks, Quinn and his squad appeared to be doing the right things. More importantly they figured out what it was like to win again after the previous season's shenanigans. Four wins from the four pre-season friendlies offered a bit of optimism, even when you put to one side the relative abilities of the opposition.

Those four away wins, all of which were without conceding a goal, may have seemed like the perfect preparation for the season and that Quinn might be have been made for this management lark. But in hindsight, the victories over Forest Green Rovers (3–0 thanks to goals from Liam Lawrence, Daryl Murphy and Dean Whitehead), Rotherham (2–0 with goals from Murphy and Jon Stead), League of Ireland outfit Shelbourne (2–0 courtesy of Murphy and Rory Delap strikes) and Carlisle United (3–0 as Stead, Lawrence and Grant Leadbitter were on the mark) were a curve ball. We have all learned by now to set little or no store by pre-season friendlies. What waited was more misery during the opening month of the Championship season and no doubt a sharp realisation from Quinn that he had to find a full-time manager to steer the ship through increasingly choppier waters. Quinn did, however, leave his club suit in the boardroom and donned his tracksuit in the dugout for the first six games of the season.

Then Sunderland centr-half, Kenny Cunningham recalls the situation: "Sunderland were training down at Bath University and I joined up with them as I was looking for a new club. Kevin Richardson was hands on at the time and there was a lot of talk of a big appointment as manager. It dragged on a bit into the season but there it was in the end. As chairman, Niall signed me. He then took on the manager's job. He was waiting to appoint a new manager, but took on the job while that was going on. He took it on but it didn't work out too well. He had a good relationship with the fans and he had the respect of the players. By virtue of the facts of the takeover, he was unable to appoint the new manager at the time; it was the obvious thing to step in.

"We lost the first game at Coventry away, which was the game I made my debut in. We lost against Plymouth, Birmingham and Southend too. It was one of those starts to a season when you think 'bloody hell' what could happen here."

Jim Fox of *Seventy3* magazine recalls that strange pre-season: "The game I remember in particular was away at Forest Green Rovers. It was played on an absolutely sweltering July day and their ground is in deepest, rural Gloucestershire (in the village of Nailsworth) so a bizarre setting anyway for a football match. Being Sunderland, we of course had hundreds of supporters there and I'm sure by the end some had succumbed to the effects of sunstroke. I'm sure alcohol was not involved.

Anyway, the game was presumably arranged because Gary Owers was then their manager. Because Forest Green's home strip is black and white stripes, Owers decided this would be completely unacceptable and made them play in their all green away kit. You couldn't make it up.

The trip to Carlisle was, shall we say, not without incident off the field both before and after the match. We took loads there on the train, as you would imagine. Despite a heavy police presence in the town, there was a fair bit of trouble beforehand as Carlisle's proximity to Newcastle might lead one to anticipate. Afterwards, all the police attention was on ensuring that our fans, for obvious reasons, did not disembark in Newcastle. I remember people being compulsorily conveyed to Heworth and Sunderland even if that wasn't where they were heading. It's something one learns to live with as a football fan. The strangest thing of all, however, was seeing Niall on the touchline and in the dugout. It just never looked right."

Coventry City 2 Sunderland 1, 6 August 2006

A Sunday televised game and a 52nd-minute strike from Murphy, who carried on his pre-season form into the opening game of the season, gave Quinn his first goal as Sunderland manager and the Black Cats the lead. It looked likely to ensure the campaign got off to the best possible start. But a line-up which featured so many of those who were humiliated in the 15-point Premier League relegation still had plenty of inadequacies that were still too prevalent. Stern John, who would, later in the season, become a Sunderland player, struck a wonder goal to level matters 19 minutes from time and, seven minutes later, a sleepy defence were caught ball watching and allowed Gary McSheffrey time and space to fire home the winner.

Quinn, acutely aware of the issues still within the camp from the nightmare previous season, reflected on his first game as a manager: "We were caught napping. That's a glitch we had last season and cost us dear again. That is something we can work on. Stern John's goal was world-class and you can do very little about something like that. But I do not want that to take away from our performance which was full of enthusiasm and for the most part, I think we outplayed Coventry."

"This was our first and so far only visit to the Ricoh Arena," remembers Jim Fox. "Because, like most or all out of town stadia, adjacent refreshment opportunities can be at a premium, we somehow ended up pre-match drinking in a backstreet working men's club behind the large *Tesco* across the car park from the ground. Fortunately, Coventry were yet to erect the statue of the diabolical Jimmy Hill which now blemishes the stadium sur-rounds. I suspect there might have been problems had it been there at the time. I'm amazed it's still standing, to be honest."

Sunderland 0 Birmingham City 1, 9 August 2006

Just 26,668 supporters turned up to the Stadium of Light to witness Quinn's first home game as manager. The performance may have given both the boss and the fans a flicker of optimism, but the reality was that the taste defeat was only too familiar. Mikael Forssell's penalty winner was perhaps not deserved on the balance of play. Quinn had clearly garnered some improvement from his players at least, but confidence in their own abil-ity was still missing from those out on the pitch. One error was all it took against Steve Bruce's Birmingham City, who eventually would appear in the home dugout some three years later and be appointed by Quinn. This time, however, the guilty party was not one of the players nursing the Premier League hangover; instead it was debutant Clive Clarke who had joined the club 24 hours earlier as part of George McCartney's transfer to West Ham. His reckless tackle late in the first-half consigned Sunderland to yet another defeat.

The ever upbeat Quinn saw some positives in his post-match comments: "I'm not as disappointed as I was on Sunday (after the defeat at Coventry) because we played for the full 90 minutes against arguably the best team in the division. The players showed me heart and it means I can now work on a bit more creativity on the training ground. That's what we lacked and I'm looking to bring in players to give us that." One of those signings followed 24 hours later in the form of Riera.

Sunderland 2 Plymouth Argyle 3, 12 August 2006

Another 2,400 or so supporters voted with their feet as the miserable run of form continued. Even despite his hero status on Wearside, Quinn was unable to find the winning formula as manager. This time, just 24,377 were at the Stadium of Light to watch newly promoted Plymouth claim a late winner in a dramatic game. It had been the perfect start for Sunderland with Daryl Murphy netting with just a minute on the clock, but just seven minutes later the scores were level again as David Norris lobbed Ben Alnwick. An injury, 20 minutes into the game to Clive Clarke required a defensive reshuffle and before the interval, Sunderland were behind as Barry Hayles struck following an error from Kenny Cunningham. Stephen Elliott's leveller midway into the second half looked like it might end the losing run, but Nick Chadwick secured the points for Plymouth eight minutes from time.

Afterwards, Quinn pulled no punches: "I'm very disappointed. It's a game we should have won. It was a wonderful chance to get going and turn a corner, but it was awful at times and we lacked bottle to take the situation by the scruff of the neck. The players have to take on responsibility and as a unit we didn't do that. Everyone and his dog know we have to strengthen the squad."

Southend 3 Sunderland 1, 19 August 2006

There was no respite for Quinn in the manager's hot seat as a fourth-straight league defeat left Sunderland bottom of the table. This time, it was newly promoted Southend who proved too hot with two goals from Adam Barrett and another strike from Lee Bradbury leaving Quinn's side 3–0 down before Jon Stead struck a last minute consolation. Arnau Riera was seen for the first time in a red and white shirt when appearing as a fifty-fifth minute substitute, but there was to be no change of fortune.

Speaking at Roots Hall, an increasingly frustrated Quinn said: "There's a percentage of players in the dressing room who are simply not good enough. We've put our arm round them and looked after them over the past few weeks, but the losing mentality is rampant in this dressing room. When you see that you realise some just aren't going to make the cut."

Bury 2 Sunderland 0, 22 August 2006

Just when Quinn thought things could not get any worse, they did just that. A League Cup tie with the Football League's bottom side was meant to be the opportunity to finally end the losing start to the season, but embarrassingly it only extended it to five games. In front of less than 3,000 fans, half of then away fans, Arnau Riera was dismissed with four minutes on the clock for an elbow in the face and 10-man Sunderland succumbed to two late goals from John Fitzgerald and Andy Bishop.

Quinn revealed afterwards that he was close to appointing a new manager, who we would find out to be Roy Keane, and relinquish his role as manager. "I'll revert back to Chairman as soon as possible. It's been hard being temporary manager. I've been working hard behind the scenes to get the manager in place. I stepped into this role because I didn't get the quality of manager I thought I would but we are now getting very close to doing that. I know my role is best here as chairman. I can't name names because we've nothing done yet but we're getting closer. We think we've somebody who will give people a big lift they need and we'll give him the budget he deserves."

Striker Stephen Elliott, who played in the game, remembers the despair in the small Gigg Lane dressing room afterwards. "I remember the Bury game, Arnau Riera had started well the previous game and in the starting few minutes he elbowed a Bury player and we were down to 10 men. The rest was all downhill and nothing went right. The dressing room was desperate (afterwards) and we knew we had let the fans and ourselves down. Niall told us that a new manager was coming but we didn't know who. It was horrible time as we were favourites to go up, but could not buy a win at that time."

Seventy3 Editor Jim Fox recalls that grim night all too clearly. "The irony, of course, was the memory of the glorious 5–2 victory on the same ground which saw us clinch promotion under Peter Reid. That recollection had turned to ashes in our mouths that night. After the game, I remember my group trudging its way from Gigg Lane back to Bury and catching the tram back into Manchester where we were spending the night. The only course of action which seemed appropriate was to find a pub which had, shall we say, flexible closing hours and hold an immediate inquest, not so much about what had gone wrong more importantly with what the hell we could do next.

Like everyone else, we had had no tip-off about the incoming manager but, as much as we loved him, it was clear Niall could not continue for much longer or a return to the land that time forgot, usually called the

Third Division, was on the cards. We really were staring into the abyss that night in *The Smithfield* in Manchester although I remember staring hard at my empty pint glass for a while when last orders were eventually called. The Keane announcement soon after, by Richard Keys on **Sky Sports News** as I recall, was a bombshell."

Sunderland 2 West Bromwich Albion 0, 28 August 2006

Two new arrivals were added to the squad as Quinn signed William Mocquet from Le Havre and Tobias Hysen from Djurgardens, the latter for £1.7 million. In a revolving door, Kevin Kyle departed to Coventry City with Quinn sanctioning his sale. But the big news in the build up to Quinn's final game in charge as temporary manager was that his successor would be Roy Keane. And, with the new man in the stands, Sunderland finally tasted victory to ensure Quinn's six-game spell in charge ended in positive fashion. Dean Whitehead scored direct from a first-half corner and Neill Collins banked the points when heading home a cross from the impressive Hysen. Quinn's toil in both the boardroom and the dugout had finally reaped some reward as he passed the baton onto Keane.

In his last post-game verdict as a manager, a beaming Quinn said: "It's a great feeling. People thought we were going to get spanked again today so for them to perform like that, I'm very proud. The manager (Keane) knows he's got characters in there. It was astonishing when you consider what they've been through. They impressed their new manager I would say. They won it the right way."

The revolving door would, of course, turn into a spinning turnstile as *Sky Sports News* (*SSN*) did its usual dramatic hype of transfer deadline day on the Thursday following the West Brom game. Jim Fox recalls that evening: "As was our habit on a Thursday in those days, we were in The Lansdowne pub off Hylton Road in Sunderland from about 8pm. Every other news story which appeared on *SSN* breaking news seemed to be another SAFC arrival. You wondered where it would end as Liam Miller; Graham Kavanagh; David Connolly; Stan Varga; Dwight Yorke and Ross Wallace were announced in rapid succession. The assumption was that the sheer force of Keane's personality had been enough to persuade all these people to join the cause but it certainly gave everyone a lift for the impending trip to Derby County on the Saturday."

"It was a strange day, that Bank Holiday Monday," recalls Fox. "It was a massive relief to win a game, of course. However, we were still in a state of shock from Keane's arrival and even though I couldn't see him sitting up in the West Stand, I'm sure everyone there and certainly the players could feel that intense stare burning into their shirts: it had the desired effect, anyway. What I will never forget are the scenes the following Saturday at Pride Park for Roy's official first game as manager. Even by our standards we had taken what seemed like an incredible away support to Derby and the mayhem behind the goal when we equalised and then quickly scored what proved to be the winner was incredible. I remember afterwards seeing pictures of Roy being mobbed as he got off the team bus although, of course, pre match refreshment duties meant I missed that episode."

New Keane signing, Graham Kavanagh also noted the away following at Derby for Keane's first game and the buzz about the place in general. "We had around five thousand supporters that day (at Derby) and it was unbelievable. We played Leeds away soon after and I scored, the atmosphere from the travelling crowd was immense. I also remember the first game at the SOL, there were hundreds of Irish banners, the belief from the fans was amazing."

BBC Five Live radio chief football correspondent Ian Dennis, a regular in the press box at the Stadium of Light, likened Quinn's reign to that of Bob Stokoe when he returned to take charge of Sunderland for a second time. "I remember in the late 80's when Bob Stokoe took over back at Sunderland and the euphoria that was generated amongst Sunderland's travelling support at one of his first games away at Bradford City. Obviously you can't compare Stokoe and Quinn as managers, but for that same magnetic esteem then Quinn would be a modern day equivalent. His record in his brief spell (as manager) was a disappointment, but I never saw him more than a stopgap option anyway. His appointment of Keane was a gamble, but it's a gamble that more than paid off."

It was time for Quinn to watch from afar and enjoy the remainder of the season in the role he had envisaged from the outset, as Chairman.

"Niall is a very bright lad," added Cunningham. "It is not easy having the chairman's hat on and Niall walked the tightrope well. He had a vision for the club and how he wanted to move it on. He played for the club and he knew how to keep a happy medium with the supporters. He's got that special manner to him. He was what the club needed and was a perfect fit. I'm not sure why he didn't put himself up to become the president of Ireland."

It would, however, not be all plain sailing for Sunderland under Keane. Promotion, if anyone was even daring to contemplate it, seemed a long way off as Christmas 2006 arrived in the wake of defeats to Ipswich, Preston, Stoke, Cardiff and Norwich. The springboard, of course, was a 2–0 New Year's Day win at Leicester which began a fifteen match unbeaten run culminating with the wonder goal of Carlos Edwards at home to Burnley and Derby's defeat at Palace which saw us promoted. Niall's big gamble had paid off after all.

The Irish revolution was in full effect on Wearside.

Chapter Four
Andy Powell and Jim Fox

Roy Keane and the Irish Revolution

It was the era of the Irish iron fist which would prove to be a vital yet enigmatic period of transformation in the life of Sunderland football club. After yet another frustrating relegation from the first tier of English football to the gloomy if nostalgic Tuesday evenings in the Championship, the season did not start the way every Mackem would ultimately have desired. With Saint Niall taking hold of the managerial reins, the club headed into the season with optimism. Why not? Niall had proven over the years that he is a born winner, a talismanic figure of achievement, success and charm; a silhouette carved from sheer class and elegance. Surely this infinite aura of success would transfer to his career as an interim manager?

Alas, his managerial skills would not run parallel to the legacy of his playing ability nor his knack for good business. The man with the red and white halo lost five of his six games in charge of the club and it was clear for all to see, including Niall himself, that managing a team and a club at the same time was a hard task to contend with. Was it down to his good nature? Was it perhaps the strain of Chairmanship? Or was it just simply that Niall Quinn was many things in life except a tactical genius?

Whatever the reason behind this small failure, Niall came out of it with his head held high and his dignity intact. He did this by knowing when to step away and, perhaps most importantly, in the decision he made during this conclusion. Remarkably the soft spoken, gentle giant was the man responsible for the appointment of the stoic, hard as nails tyrant who was known in every corner of the football world, Roy Keane.

It started with a promise of a world class manager and ended in a plethora of questions, deadwood signings and most importantly, that terrible feeling we as Black Cat fans feel too often… desolation and angst as to what will happen next. It could be suggested that sentence could sum up Keane's era perfectly but that would be unfair because his time at Sunderland – although expensive – was more important than that.

Keane officially took charge on Tuesday 29 of August 2006 when he was unveiled by Quinn. Niall went on record to state that: "This represents a major coup for our football club." A world class manager had been promised and a world class manager had then been expected by the faithful but what we got instead was a world class footballer. The question was does one guarantee the other? It would be naïve to answer that upon first glimpse but it was a question that would be solved over the next three years of Keane's contract.

While Roy was one of football's true greats, there could be no guarantee he was cut from the same managerial cloth as people like Sir Alex Ferguson and Brian Clough, whom he had worked under during his spectacular playing career. After all, look at Niall Quinn and his ill-fated half dozen games in charge. But this was Roy Keane, the tough midfield enforcer who had carved out a glory laden legacy in the midfield of the most decorated team of the English game under the leadership of one the greatest managers in the history of football, Sir Alex Ferguson. Would he emulate his old master's mentality and success? Was he now destined for greatness in the Stadium of Light hot seat? Every Sunderland fan certainly hoped so!

There was no disputing the buzz in Sunderland when the news broke that Keane was to be the new manager. A feeling of 'this is it, this is right, things are finally moving forward for us this time' swirled inside the majority of fans and this transferred into the atmosphere in Niall Quinn's last game in charge. The fixture happened to be against a decent West Bromwich Albion side arriving at the SOL with the wounded beast of our football team in their sights after a five game winless streak. Albion fans would most certainly have expected three points that day but we had a different plan. This day and the win that came with it was a huge day for Sunderland AFC and it can be looked at as an important turning point in our history.

I remember the day well. The SOL was buzzing with excitement yet a nervy anticipation bubbled underneath it all. Knowing Roy Keane was in the crowd and chomping at the bit to take full control stirred everyone up, buoyed spirits and lifted not only the entire club but the city as a whole.

The atmosphere was electric. A current ran through the crowd, conducted inside of each of us in the circuit of the adjoined fan base, powered by the battery of the Keano effect.

90 minutes and two goals later we ended the day with our first three points of the season in the bag. Relief poured over the SOL in nothing short of a deluge. The terrible run had been halted and the future looked bright. If Roy Keane could have this influence on the team from the stands then it stood to reason he would have a much greater effect while in charge, commanding the players and it was enough to whet the appetite of the fans. Although somewhat a tyrant in persona, his respected reputation would instill dedication and diligence from the team and make individuals stand up and be counted, much like we saw against West Brom. The Keano effect was, we all hoped, the perfect ingredient needed to bring to life the potion of our squad.

Exciting times were ahead and to encourage this belief, Sunderland fans were treated to a remarkable deadline day transfer rampage. Fans from all over the country can relate to the excitement of the final day of the transfer window. The unknown, the surprises that spring into view via the *Sky Sports News* yellow ticker and the anticipation to see who may join and who may leave the club all adds up to create quite the spectacle. At the end of August 2006, Black Cat fans would be treated to an electric evening of non-stop activity.

In a flurry to put his own touch on the squad he had inherited, Keane signed several players before the window slammed shut. In came former Manchester United team mates Dwight Yorke and Liam Miller in addition to former Celtic players Ross Wallace and Stanislav Varga (Varga's second time at Sunderland having been signed back in 2000 by Peter Reid). Irish internationals Graham Kavanagh and David Connolly would also join the cause, coming straight from the Irish training camp as Graham Kavangh told *Seventy3* Magazine. "I was in the Irish squad and we were playing away to Germany on deadline day in 2006, when the call came from Paul Jewell (then Wigan boss) saying 'Sunderland want you'. He didn't have to ask twice and the lure of joining Roy Keane's team was too much for me. I left the Irish camp and headed for Sunderland.

I went from Germany in the morning and was at Dublin airport awaiting a connection, when in walks a surprised Liam Miller, whom was also at the Irish camp. We exchanged comments of 'what you doing here?' and we both said 'I am going to Sunderland'. We were both dead keen to sign and knew this was going to be special.

Quinn had just taken over and it was a very slow start to the Championship, but I always felt that if Keane could get it right that it could be amazing and I was greatly excited to get the chance to join. I really wanted to know his (Keane) training methods and how he was going to be as manager."

Back in Sunderland, I remember sitting in front of the TV that evening watching with intense scrutiny as the signings rolled it. It felt like it was non-stop on the transfer front and that I was watching the reshaping of the team right before my eyes in a single evening. I cannot think of another evening like it in terms of excitement, surprise and consistency.

Within days, Roy Keane had already put his own stamp on the squad. With so many new faces coming in at the same time it was always going to be a gamble. The actions of the inexperienced manager could easily blow up in his face but that was a risk he was willing to take and, ultimately, a risk that paid off.

In return for our free spending, we gained a wealth of experience which was vital in the goal of avoiding relegation into the abyss of League One. Survival was the realistic target that year because descent into another league – especially so soon after relegation from the Premier league – would have been devastating for the club. Any fan would have been happy just to guarantee our position in the Championship with a view of seeking promotion in the next season. What we got however was something quite remarkable. The conclusion of a season that started in turmoil would end in one of the closest things to a miracle the country had witnessed in football.

Winning the championship that year was, in my opinion, Roy Keane's biggest achievement in his career. Forget everything he accomplished as a Red Devil. Topping the Championship was an unbelievable feat in his first season and even more so when you consider the circumstances of his arrival. The Keano effect was applied in force and the club benefited from it more than many fans would like to admit. This integral season is a huge, monumental era in our history and one that should not be overlooked. The alternatives could have been much worse. Imagine if we had slipped out of the Championship and into the chasm of the lower leagues? Imagine if we then continued in descent of the same slippery slope? Such a slope has already devoured many teams throughout recent years, none of whom seem like they will recover from it any time soon. Keane's appointment stopped the rot and boosted us and that is what makes his time at the helm so important in our history and so underrated, most likely the most underrated achievement for Sunderland AFC since Denis Smith guided the club at the first attempt from the old Third Division in 1988 – the club's lowest ebb, but one that needed addressing and quick.

That season we stormed to the top of the Championship with some fantastic performances and even better results. The players in the squad remained motivated throughout the campaign and put their best efforts into the red and white shirt. The experience Yorke brought to the squad – although mainly within the dressing room – also played a big part in the mentality throughout the season. He complimented Keane as the link between the players and the manager and in some respects he played the proverbial 'good cop' in the 'good cop – bad cop' routine.

Speaking of Yorke, Keane's appointment at Ipswich in 2009, three years later, prompted a fair bit of analysis of the Cork man's record at Sunderland, in particular of his somewhat "shopaholic" tendencies. This was understandable given that in less than two and a half seasons at the helm at the Stadium of Light, Roy managed to spend no less than £80 million on thirty-nine players. Roy's achievement in winning the Championship and keeping Sunderland up are not in doubt but is the balance sheet on his signings in the red or the black?

The worry in the media was that Roy might not find Ipswich Town's pockets to be as deep as those at Sunderland. In fairness to Roy, his immediate target was to attract to the club players capable of enabling Sunderland to survive in the Premiership. He was then faced with the daunting task of keeping the club in the top flight after an unexpected and some would say premature promotion.

Some would argue about whether one can achieve promotion too early but Roy knew he needed new talent to survive and then, in the summer of 2008, added more or less an entire new squad which probably featured more failures than successes.

Looking first at Roy's successful signings, it could be argued that the free transfer signing of his old mate Dwight Yorke from Sydney was the shrewdest. Dwight, in the midfield role he was by now enjoying at international level, not only helped to ensure Sunderland's Premier League status but also helped to enliven Tyneside nightlife during his stay. Age, of course, caught up with him but he did exactly what he was brought in to do at the time.

The two loan spells Jonny Evans enjoyed at the club made him a long-term favourite with the fans even if hopes, and attempts, to sign him permanently were always doomed to flounder on the rocks of Ferguson's shrewdness and well-known admiration for the Irish youngster who would go to play regularly in the Old Trafford first team. Some of us with connections in Manchester had been hearing for years about the prodigious talent lurking in Ferguson's youth side and we were not to be disappointed. Don't forget Evans was even able to make Nosworthy look like a decent player at times.

Anton Ferdinand was a surprise £8 million signing from West Ham, the surprise being that he was thought to be one of those players, in the Defoe mould, very reluctant to leave London. Forever in the shadow of his brother, there were doubts about him but it is probably fair to say that by the time he inevitably returned to London with QPR, he was held in high esteem by most fans on Wearside.

I am classing the loan signing of Djibril Cisse as a success if only for the fact that he liked scoring against Newcastle. We were surprised when he came and never expected him to stay, despite what he said about Quinn reneging on the offer of a permanent deal. It was fun, and colourful, while it lasted. He's also the Lord of Frodsham which has to be a winner.

Two relatively short-term successes were Kenwyne Jones and Andy Reid. Jones would eventually leave but not for Tottenham, as seemed likely at one time, but the Potteries and Stoke City in a strangely structured deal payment-wise. Only signed because Mido chose Middlesbrough, Jones started well but, stereotypically, his attitude was questionable and his star has waned considerably at Stoke, the arrival of Crouch meaning the writing was on the wall. A swap deal with Tottenham for a certain Darren Bent had seemed on the cards at one time but we will draw a veil over that player now.

The folk-singing, guitar-playing Reid might have looked like a pub player but the affable Irishman made many friends whilst at the Stadium of Light and his touch and skill was welcome. He is likely always to be fondly remembered for that wonderful injury-time volleyed winner at home to West Ham which went a long way towards ensuring our survival in 2008.

Looking at the other successes of Roy's shopping frenzy; I will court controversy here by naming Magpie Danny Simpson as an effective loan signing who, at the time, helped the unlikely promotion push in 2007. I would also class Marton Fulop as a success in terms of his modest fee, resale value and capable stand-in performances for the unfortunate Craig Gordon.

Two other ex Manchester United staff must also count as successes. The first is Kieran Richardson for whom we not only recouped a good fee on his move to Fulham in the summer of 2012 but who, having found God already, became immortal when he scored the winner against Newcastle in 2008 – Sunderland's first home victory over their local rivals for 28 years. Kieran was frustrating because one saw in flashes that he was capable of so much more but I think we had our £5.5M worth of value from him.

Scottish international Phil Bardsley is judged a success overall and must have been bemused when Pascal Chimbonda, of whom more later, arrived at Sunderland. Phil was reliable and committed, rather than inspiring. He will be remembered for his goal at Goodison Park in the 2011–12 FA Cup Sixth round which created the fleeting illusion that we might actually beat Everton one day and edge ever closer to silverware.

Speaking of Craig Gordon, news in February 2012 of his likely retirement from the game through injury looks like bringing to a close a frustrating and disappointing career which looked so full of potential when we signed him from Hearts. In hindsight, the then record fee for a keeper of £9 million was madness on Keane's part. He was competent and sought-after and had international caps but, let's face it, he was Scottish and played in goal so work it out for yourself.

Carlos Edwards was also injury-plagued but counts as a success for his impact in the promotion run-in. Nobody present will forget his vital Easter goal at Southampton and, of course, that Friday night screamer at home to Burnley which got us promoted. Carlos is still at Ipswich and has probably found his level, sadly.

Dickson Etuhu would eventually come good at Premier League level at Fulham under Roy Hodgson but, having paid £1.5 million for him to Norwich, he started well as a midfield destroyer figure but fizzled out by Christmas of 2007.

Steed Malbranque could be inconsistent and frustrating but he's a success because, well, he's Belgian or French or, who cares, the fans loved him and could shout "STEEEEEEED" in a way which could only amuse football fans. He arrived as part of the still odd looking Spurs transfer trio but was a major hit compared to the other two, not that that was hard with "Sick Note Teemu" and "Le Sulk Pascal".

The success of a signing, of course, depends on whether it is viewed as one to keep us in, or get us out of the Championship, or secure Premier League status. Sunderland had tried and failed to sign David Connolly years previously. When he finally arrived for around £1.4 million from Wigan, finishing as the leading scorer in the Championship must count as a success. However, he was unlikely to figure in the Premier League and injury meant we could not move him on.

The list of Roy's transfer hits may seem small considering how many people he bought; a turnstile rather than a door on the Academy seemed appropriate at one time. We must now turn our attention to the roll-call of shame, the inventory of ignominy and, sadly, it's a case of where do we start?

Liam Miller was signed on a free from, of course, Manchester United. Despite being a fixture in Trapattoni's Ireland squad, he could not hold down a starting berth under Roy and went out on loan. The career highlight with Sunderland was a scorcher away at Middlesbrough.

Many would count Graham Kavanagh a success but I don't. Another Championship level footballer who briefly did a job that was needed at the time, a likeable character and proved popular with the fans, but Kav suffered from injury and was only ever a short-term acquisition before prolonging his career at Carlisle United.

Stan Varga was very popular, largely based on a storming original debut performance, but was quickly found out at Premier League Level, the SPL whence he came being about his standard. Ross Wallace, tellingly, is still playing in the Championship with Burnley but ended up leaving Sunderland to go on loan to Preston. He is fondly remembered for his stoppage-time winner at Hull City and, whilst never Premier League standard, had looked set for the dubious honour of Scottish caps at one point.

Although he started off well at the home of football, Stoke City, we signed Danny Higginbotham from them for a decent fee mainly because, you've guessed it, he used to play for Manchester United. The writing was on the wall once Jonny Evans appeared and he returned to the Potteries. Who wouldn't? Higginbotham did once score in a north-east Derby against Newcastle so not all bad.

Amongst the names I have tried, but failed, to forget are: Lewin Nyatanga, a loan signing at left-back who quickly demonstrated that you don't have to be very good to be a Welsh international and soon headed back to Derby whence he came. Remember the memorably named Stern John? He ended up on loan at Bristol City and was used as a makeweight in the Kenwyne Jones deal. He was clearly not good enough but, in fairness, scored a few key goals in the promotion push, notable one at West Brom in a 2–1 win in which Yorke was the other marksman.

Teemu Tainio was one of the Spurs triumvirate but injuries meant we never got to find out how useful he could have been to us.

Painful as it is, duty behoves us to mention the waste of potential that was Anthony Stokes. As with Gordon, we were seduced by the apparent notion that doing well in Scotland counts for something. There was jubilation when we fended off keen competition from Charlton, West Ham and Celtic to sign him for £2 million and even more joy amongst the pubs and clubs of Wearside when it quickly became apparent that business was booming when he was around. Stokes might be kindly said to have had some behavioural issues and ended up at Celtic, his level, after several loan spells. He is best remembered for a last minute winner at home to Derby and err... missing the team bus on an away day outing, which did not impress Keane.

I once had dinner with Paul McShane and he was a thoroughly pleasant and charming young man. Unfortunately, having signed from WBA for £2.5 million, he will always be remembered for a certain drubbing at Goodison Park (7–1 under Keane) and a sending off at the Emirates. He went on loan to Hull and ended up there whilst, typically, being a regular member of the Republic of Ireland squad. Like many, no lack of commitment but lacking in quality and too prone to errors.

David Meyler has recently decided to hitch his wagon to the Steve Bruce promotion party piece at Hull City. Roy must have felt sorry for Cork City and did them a favour when he signed him. He was desperately unlucky with injury but, as we know, the Premier League is unforgiving and he was never good enough at that level.

Bafflingly, we paid West Ham £4.5 million to get George McCartney back: Paul of Beatles fame, would probably have been more use given George's lack of form and injuries. They love him at West Ham but few tears were shed when he went to dirty Leeds on loan. Remember George is a Northern Ireland international which is about the same as being a San Marino international.

Moving on from mere failures, such as Ian Harte who came back to haunt us in February 2013, it's now time to look at unmitigated disasters amongst Roy Keane's signings.

Pascal Chimbonda, one of the so-called "Tottenham Three" with Tainio and Malbranque, could not have more clearly spelt trouble had he arrived wearing a T shirt saying "I am trouble, do not sign me". Roy was undeterred, however, and got the trouble everyone expected. He was an utter waste of time of whom it was said he had "timekeeping" and attitude issues.

Whilst we are on the subject of trouble as in "mad as a box of frogs", what could possibly go wrong with signing El-Hadji Diouf from Bolton for £2.5 million? Tough guy Roy thought he could handle him but Sigmund Freud would have given up on this nutcase. Roy left and so did "El-Hadji the Radgie", to Blackburn.

Let's remember Rade Prica, shall we? I thought not. He was a £2 million January panic signing from Aalborg and memorably scored at home to Birmingham. He was soon on his way back to Sweden and it is doubtful how anyone thought him capable of playing in the Premier League.

Nick Colgan was no doubt a nice lad but nobody knew why we signed him when we had Carson on the books: a pointless addition to the wage bill. Speaking of baffling signings, how about £300,000 to Paris St Germain for Jean-Yves Mvoto? Who? Who indeed? There was never a hope of him getting near the first team.

Another completely pointless signing was David Healy. Why? It's because when we signed him we already had nine, count them, strikers on our books. We should have given up on him eighteen months earlier when we tried to get him from Leeds. He spent virtually all his time on the bench: a waste of money. He's a Northern Ireland legend, of course: enough said.

Reading are believed still to be laughing at the thought of the reported £2.5 million Greg Halford cost Sunderland for the eight hopeless appearances he made. I remember him ending up at Sheffield United and, against all odds, he is believed still to be earning a living as a professional footballer. He was alleged to have "issues", the main one being a complete lack of ability.

I was incredulous when I heard we were trying to sign Michael Chopra from Cardiff City in relation to his Geordie roots, even more so than when Lee Clark arrived from Newcastle. Once again, the folly of signing "one of them" from up the road was brutally demonstrated in the infamous moment at the Sports Direct Arena when Chopra contrived to somehow fluff a winning goal chance against his mates and hometown team in a north-east Derby representing Sunderland. Why did we expect anything different? To make matters worse, we paid an incredible £5 million for this "goal poacher" then played him on the wing! A dark and shameful stain on the club's history ended when we got most of our money back from Cardiff. He has been in the news recently, bringing back to memory the hoary old Stan Bowles joke about "if only he could pass a bookies the way he passes a ball". In summary a leopard never changes his spots, in this case his stripes of a football team, causing in turn a paranoia factor for both sets of fans from the two north-east clubs (Middlesbrough after all is in North York-shire) should any of us try to sign a player with a past for either side's rivals – hence the plethora of sceptism, when Steve Bruce arrived as manager, but more of that later.

Researching this chapter, I have come across people I had almost forgot-ten had been on the books so many did Roy sign and so insignificant was their contribution to the cause. To be honest, it's a wonder Roy's tenure is remembered as the undoubted success it was when you look back.

For example, apart from helping out an old mate, what possessed us to sign Andy, sorry Andrew, Cole and what did he think he would add to his CV by coming here? Like Meyler, we did Cork another favour by signing Roy O'Donovan. We had low expectations of Roy and he more than lived down to them.

Whilst on the subject of useless players from the Celtic fringes, remem-ber Russell Anderson? No, I thought you wouldn't. We gave Aberdeen £1 million for him: nobody knows why. He played one game for us, as a sub-stitute, before going on loan, in between regular injuries, to Burnley and Plymouth.

Perhaps, a contributing factor to the amount of transfer activity from Keane, was down to his Chairman, allowing him such space to manoeuvre in the transfer market. No doubt, the cards would have been laid on the table when Keane walked through the doors at the SOL, that it would be his way and no other way, otherwise he would walk.

This presumption could somewhat be reinforced, when Keane did walk, but only when Quinn had passed the mantle of power to the incoming Ellis Short, who purchased 30% of the Drumaville shares on 25 September 2008. Only when Short questioned Keane's whereabouts during the week leading up to games, did Roy feel his feet being trodden on and walked away.

Quinn though would have provided assurance to Keane that such micro management as it could be deemed in some quarters would not happen under his watch and this approach worked, until the choppier waters of the Premier League were reached, Sunderland struggled and only then were the first questions asked. Who knows what may have happened, if

Roy was not the instant success he turned out to be, would Quinn have posed the right questions to the rookie manager?

Well, there you have it. It's more a revolving door than a transfer merry-go-round with Roy but you can't say there was ever a dull moment. Despite making fun of Roy's rubbish deals, let us not forget the miracle he achieved in getting us up and keeping us up. Who would have thought on 25 October 2008 when he became the first Sunderland manager to beat Newcastle at home in over twenty-eight years that a 1–4 home defeat to Bolton a month later would see his departure. It would all go sour again at Portman Road but who is to say he won't be tempted to try his hand again? We owe him a lot but Chimbonda; come on Roy?

Chapter Five

Black Cat Down – The Story of Niall Quinn's Taxi Cabs

Jim Fox

"Niall Quinn's taxi cabs are the best,
So stick it up your a*** Easyjet,
Fat Freddie wouldn't do it for the Mags,
Niall Quinn's taxi cabs!"
– Hastily adapted fans' anthem of the 2006–07 season

Niall Quinn wasn't your average football club Chairman. Nothing epitomised the unique relationship he enjoyed with we Sunderland fans better than the bizarre events on the evening of 31 March 2007 which unfolded at Bristol airport and which, to this day, seem surreal even though I was a participant in, and eye-witness to, an episode embedded in the folklore of all those who follow Sunderland.

Niall's immortal quote that night, which still makes the spine tingle, was of course "These are my people!" and in the unlikely surroundings of the departures hall at Bristol airport, he became our Mandela, our Gandhi and our Martin Luther King rolled into one. We would have done anything he asked or told us to do that night. Had he told us to line up in twos, hold hands and set off to walk home we probably would have done it. Something special happened that night. As one fan interviewed by the *Sunderland Echo* told the late Ian Laws, he loved Quinny so much he would give him a kidney but then changed his mind. "The bloke's a legend," he declared, "he can have both of my kidneys."

Before recreating the events of that night, it is wise to place them in context and try to explain their irony. By this I mean that although there was initial disbelief back home as the news of what had happened spread, in many ways those of us present were less surprised once the immediate shock of how we were being treated wore off. After all, he might have been one of our heroes who now had the fate of our cherished team in his hands but he was one of us first and foremost. He was a fan like us, albeit a VIP fan. You don't desert your mates when they need you and he came through when we needed him in the most practical way possible.

The events are now the stuff of legend. In short, Niall made sure around eighty Sunderland fans got home safely after their flight was unjustly cancelled by a paranoid pilot unable to distinguish between enthusiasm and disorder. This involved the commandeering of what seemed like every taxi in the greater Bristol area, eighteen in total, at a cost of approximately £8,000. The journey home averaged over 300 miles. Would any other Chairman have done this?

Can we imagine Abramovic commandeering a squadron of Lear jets to rescue stranded Chelsea supporters or perhaps an idle Etihad jumbo jet swooping in to get Man City home? These ideas are unthinkable so removed from the fan in the street are the moguls now controlling the modern day football club.

The football club chairman as ex-player, emergency manager, kit man and travelling fan was certainly a deviation from the normal persona of football Chairman. At one time, the typical chairman was the self-made local businessman who ran the club as his personal fiefdom. The best example of this would probably be the Bob Lord era at Burnley of the sixties and seventies. Whilst this type of chairman's ambition might not have extended beyond having the main stand named after him, the transformation wrought at Blackburn by Jack Walker represented a quantum leap in ambition. Home grown tycoons like Walker are now, of course, considered paupers on the international football ownership scale.

Nowadays, when even our own club is owned by a reclusive Texan billionaire and Premier League clubs are the routine playthings of petrochemical oligarchs and Arab Sheikhs, it is worth remembering that Niall's figurehead role at the apex of the Drumaville consortium was motivated solely by his love of our club and the wish to see it back in the top echelon of the game. What the club meant to him was more than amply demonstrated that early spring night on the outskirts of Bristol.

Three wins out of four in March saw a healthy support make the long and unappetising trip to Wales for what was never looked on as an easy fixture, on or off the pitch, Cardiff City away. As was normal then, and is the norm now for trips to Swansea, affordable flights from Ponteland airport to Bristol with *Easyjet* connecting with the short train ride from Bristol appealed to many of our supporters, myself and my friends included.

The outbound flight was uneventful, unsurprising given the early check-in time, and we were duly delivered to the principality by around 10am. As always in Cardiff, discretion was the better part of valour and pre-match refreshment was taken, as usual, in the Cathedral Road area near the Glamorgan cricket ground. The next time we play there, the *Beverley Hotel* and *Cayo Arms*, the latter ironically Welsh speaking, may prove good options. There are certainly many pubs in Cardiff you would be wise to avoid.

The feeling was that this was a pivotal game and that a victory could well give us the momentum we needed to push on through the vital April fixtures and pull off what had seemed unthinkable on that dark night in Bury only eight months before. The arrival of Roy Keane however, in the immediate aftermath of that League Cup defeat, meant that as the business end of the season loomed, hopes were high and expectations raised. Despite never being brilliant, it had gradually become apparent that the collection of players Keane had gathered, mainly on that incredible transfer deadline night in August when we seemed to activate the *Sky Sports News* tickertape every five minutes, was actually the best in the Championship.

The game was as tight and tense as one would have expected but a seventy-second minute free-kick from Ross Wallace, aided by some suspect goalkeeping, proved enough to see off the Bluebirds.

The feeling of euphoria which followed was surpassed only by the usual feelings of relief as the train left Cardiff and one realised, once again, that you were leaving Wales for England in one piece. By the way, if this sounds exaggerated, you clearly have not been to Ninian Park. Sunderland AFC has not yet visited Cardiff's new stadium but, although less harrowing reports seem to be emerging from fans visiting now, it remains not a place to take risks. Ask anyone who has mistakenly nipped into the Ninian Park Arms for a quick pre-match pint.

The previous visit to Cardiff, a two nil win with goals from Lawrence and Whitehead was fairly uneventful as I remember. However, the one prior to that, a four nil reverse on the day John Charles died was not, being notable for the presence of what might be tactfully described as a healthy deterrent force from Wearside, robust enough to deter even Cardiff fans.

As I recall, the return flight to Ponteland (Easyjet flight EZY576) was scheduled for 21.25 hours so there was ample time to celebrate the victory in Bristol before obtaining taxis to deliver us to the airport for check-in and what we assumed would be a routine journey home: how little we realised what lay ahead.

Once at the airport, the mood in the bar was naturally buoyant, a now realistic promotion bid lying before us. It became apparent that the players had returned on an earlier flight but dozens of fans mingled happily with club officials, ordinary passengers and local journalists, the *Echo's* Graeme Anderson and the late Ian Laws included, as flight time approached.

Niall's fondness for a pint or two of Guinness was well known to say the least and he duly appeared in the bar area to a rousing greeting and a deluge of well-wishers trying to get him a pint. It has to be emphasised that not even the most sensitive and paranoid of travellers could have been at all intimidated by the atmosphere which was relaxed and comfortable if a trifle boisterous.

To emphasise this, the *Sunderland Echo* reported a passenger called Michael Braithwaite, hailing from Wearside but who had not attended the game, as saying: "There was a bit of boisterous behaviour in the queue before people boarded the plane, but a policewoman had a word with a couple of people and that should have been (the situation) dealt with. A few people had had a drink, yes, but it was a happy atmosphere and I didn't see any aggression or abuse." It hardly sounds as though a riot was in the offing, does it?

A rousing chorus of "Niall Quinn's Disco Pants" whilst we were in the queue for the bus to the plane seemed entirely harmless to those joining in and, indeed, I recall the anthem proving amusing and anything but alarming to the surrounding passengers. Those singing immediately complied with a request from the crew to settle down but I did notice the *Easyjet* check-in ground crew muttering amongst themselves and pointing at people but thought little of it as we boarded the plane and took our seats. I should have guessed that there was trouble ahead, however, when one fan was escorted from the queue and out of the departures area despite any apparent offence having been committed.

There are two distinct versions of what happened next on board the plane: the truth and the *Easyjet* version of events. The delay in take-off caused little alarm given the nature of such things. It was only when I noticed the cabin crew singling out individuals, seemingly at random, followed by the sight through the window of the hold luggage being unloaded from the plane that reality dawned on us. We weren't going to be flying anywhere this night, it appeared.

The presence of *Sunderland Echo* journalists certainly helped give some perspective to what really happened that night. Again I quote from the edition of 2 April 2007 in which 53-year-old grandmother and fan Carol Dennis of Chester-Le-Street gave her reaction to being told to leave the plane: "I couldn't believe it. I started crying and asked why I was being singled out. They said I'd pressed the call button (an offence?) but I'd done nothing of the sort. They threw off one lad who was sitting asleep causing no problems and they picked out a lad who has learning difficulties. *Easyjet* totally over-reacted and I won't be using them again. I don't know what any of us would have done without Quinny. He's a saint."

Bullies, of course, love easy targets so it was no surprise that a grandmother and a disabled person, amongst others, were singled out as scapegoats to justify the airline's use of excessive and disproportionate response. Mrs Dennis continued: "I feel embarrassed because I'm a Sunderland supporter and we don't want to be associated with this kind of thing. People who weren't there will blame drunk football fans but Niall would not have helped everyone as he did if he thought we were troublemakers."

I am not suggesting that our fans are saints to a man or that, on occasion, misbehaviour does not occur but the point about the value we place on our good reputation is well made.

As soon as flashing blue lights outside on the tarmac appeared, followed by perhaps twelve individuals being escorted from the aircraft, including as stated one disabled lad with a prosthetic limb, a spontaneous "one off, all off" movement led by Niall began to be followed by the announcement that the flight was being cancelled as there was a "threat to the security of the flight."

Despite this outrageous provocation, I remember my fellow passengers and I leaving the plane in an orderly manner and gathering back in the terminal building to decide on our best course of action. I rang my wife at this point to be told that the flight status had been showing as "cancelled" for some considerable time on the internet despite us having been told a blatant lie by the pilot, this being that the delay in the flight leaving was caused by the captain "checking some paperwork" prior to departure. This, of course, is another blatant example of the prejudice which justifies treating football fans as scum without any human rights or even the intelligence to realise that they are being treated as idiots.

Before describing the amazing events which then ensued, it is worth stating that there is one significant discrepancy in one important detail of the events of that night which may well have had a bearing on what transpired. The late Ian Laws, no doubt in good faith knowing his integrity, reported in the *Echo* that the plane having been emptied "*Easyjet* officials, via a police officer, offered to reimburse passengers for any accommodation costs involved in having to stay in Bristol and arranged alternative Sunday flights for some passengers."

The full *Easyjet* version of events was as follows: "*Easyjet* has a zero-tolerance policy towards any unacceptable behaviour onboard or towards its staff and the flight was consequently cancelled. The airline offered those passengers not involved a free transfer onto the next available flight and hotel accommodation and would like to apologise for any inconvenience caused to them."

Niall himself, as well as "vehemently opposing the airline's view that there was disruptive behaviour on board the plane" told the *Echo*: "We also deny the airline's claim that overnight accommodation was offered and this was witnessed by several independent parties." Well, who's version of events do you believe?

Meanwhile, back inside the terminal, another strange event caught the eye. Assuming *Easyjet* and Somerset and Avon Constabulary attributed the alleged problems to alcohol-fuelled and football related disorder, would one not have expected the first action the police would have taken to have been to shut the airport bar? No, astonishingly, the bar was still open and quite happy to serve us whilst we pondered our options for the night. I don't think how odd this was dawned on many people until later given the customary demonization of football fans where alcohol is concerned. I must admit, I thought "what the hell" and had another drink.

I put this apparent conundrum to a bemused police officer who, despite being dressed in riot gear, expressed doubt at having been called to the airport to deal with an alleged "riot" which was clearly nothing of the sort. "Closing the bar? We never thought of that" he confessed to me, "I can't see any problem here anyway". I advised him to express his concerns to the airline regarding the waste of police time and resources but I am not optimistic that this would have happened.

I also remember asking the puzzled policeman if he realised how lucky they were to have Sunderland fans to deal with. He didn't grasp the obvious meaning so I had to explain that whilst we were reasonable people who would comply unquestioningly with any orders given to us by our leader Niall, other fans of shall we say a more dubious reputation might not have taken things so calmly. What I actually said was "What would you have done if this had been Leeds or Millwall here?" I think even he then realised what I was on about.

I believe a few of our fans decided to head back into Bristol to seek hotels and head home by train the next morning. However, Niall quickly grasped the baton of leadership, gathering everyone together, calling for calm and order and delivering the now famous speech some of which can be seen via *YouTube*. This was Niall at his most statesman like and impressive and the respectful applause which greeted his exhortation to us to "stay together" and "we'll all get home" is something none of us there will ever forget.

Niall is a natural optimist and I remember speaking to him before he addressed us. As may be heard in the video clip, his initial response was that a couple of coaches was the most practical way of getting more than eighty people home with minimum fuss. Once it became clear that hiring coaches at eleven pm on a Saturday night was a tad ambitious, what seemed an equally unlikely plan to simply hire taxis to get every-one home was hatched. However, to Niall it was simple: it's an airport so they have a taxi rank so we just hire them all. Simple, eh?

The initial incredulity which the plan engendered soon gave way to hope as it became clear that our leader was deadly serious and would not be deterred by mere details.

One would have thought that a guarantee of payment from the Chair-man and officials of a big football club would have been enough to sat-isfy the Bristol Airport taxi company but far from it. Incredibly, they insisted on full payment for eighteen vehicles at an average of nearly £500 each being made upfront. This, I think, was finally achieved by a combination of the credit cards of Niall and several others, notably my mate and local business guru Paul Callaghan. I remember the unique sight of Niall and others queuing at the cash machines in the airport ter-minal to withdraw as much as they could to facilitate our mass exodus north.

Even in the midst of this apparent chaos, there was order. By this I mean that once the first taxis began to pull up outside the terminal, negotiations and payment having been concluded, there was no free for all. Instead, those in most need, the eldest, youngest and most distressed were prioritised and dispatched first. I don't remember what time I left but Ian Laws reported that "at 12.50am, I joined three fans I had never previously met and started on the road home. Quinn was still waiting to go. He'd make sure everyone else was sorted out first." What a man!

By pure chance, I ended up in a cab with a lad I didn't know, a lad with whom I used to work called Keith Chapman (you may know him from his contributions to the official programme) and my mate from the Royal Navy, Paul Gerry. Apart from a toilet and refreshment break, probably somewhere in the Midlands, my recollections of the epic trek back are sketchy so I must have slept most of the way back. It had been a long and memorable day, one of those genuine "I was there" days.

We must have left the airport around midnight because by around 4.30 in the morning, we were approaching Durham on the A1. One of the problems in getting everyone home from Bristol was, of course, the cosmopolitan nature of our support. By this I mean that whereas some clubs would have had 90% of people from the club's base, we have fans everywhere in the UK and, particularly, everywhere from Billingham to Blyth. There had been no way to co-ordinate each taxi taking passengers back to Durham, South Shields or Northumberland so I assume it was up to each taxi contingent to negotiate a practical drop-off route for their driver. There had been no conditions imposed like only dropping off in Sunderland, for example, however practical and reasonable these would have been as an alternative to spending the night in Bristol.

As Paul and I were resident in Derwentside, our party agreed that we two would disembark in Durham City and get home by a further taxi allowing the cabbie to then drop off in Sunderland and South Shields.

So it was that two bedraggled *Easyjet* victims waved goodbye to a Bristol taxi in Millburngate and were lucky enough to flag down a local one to get us back to Stanley and Consett for the sum of £35. The cabbie, unsurprisingly, was a little reluctant at that time of the morning to take two burly blokes but was reassured that we could afford the fare when we revealed that the taxi which he had just seen us leaving had come from Bristol! We left our explanation at that but one bizarre detail I do remember from the second, somewhat shorter taxi ride was that as soon as we left Durham the cabbie began to regale us with the difficulties of his marriage and what a difficult customer "our lass" was. I suppose it's the sort of conversation one has at 4.45 in the morning.

Even allowing for the stoical professionalism of the British taxi driver, the reaction of the cabbies that night was remarkable. It's not every Saturday night shift at the airport that your radio comes to life instructing you to embark on a midnight six hundred mile round trip. Nonetheless, as far as I know, the odyssey was treated as just another fare, albeit one they would never forget.

One nice touch that night was that quite a few grateful fans, realising that the driver would of course need a break before embarking on the return leg, insisted on the driver coming into their homes for tea, breakfast, a nap or whatever was needed. This was in stark contrast to the treatment meted out to us earlier in the evening by *Easyjet*. Anyway, a few wives and family members must have come downstairs that morning to find a stranger with a West Country accent at the breakfast table.

By the time I got to bed and came round the next day, probably around dinnertime, the news had spread on the internet and the media storm had begun and the rest, as they say, is history. Cynics will argue that it was worth the cost to Niall and the club in terms of public relations value but you won't find anyone involved that night whose mind that thought crossed. What I do know from local TV news coverage of the time was that no harm at all was done to season ticket sales which were going well at the time anyway due to our promotion surge.

I seem to remember fans queuing at the ticket office on the Monday morning being unanimous in their assessment of Sunderland being unique in having a Chairman prepared to go to such lengths for the fans. One said "he's a heart on his sleeve guy and the club is in his heart".

By Monday, "Black Cat Down" as the episode had been christened was big local and national news. One of the best media interviews, filmed outside the Stadium of Light, was given by well-known fan Steve Dean of South Shields. This is also still available on *YouTube* if you're interested and it gives a good flavour of the sense of injustice we all felt that night.

Returning to the journey home from the airport, one taxi did not make it back thus depriving one unfortunate taxi driver of a record fare. The cab which fell by the wayside happened to contain four of my friends with whom I had attended the game, two Callaghans and legendary fan Davey "Wild Man of Roker" Dowell and Brian "Taff's Tours" Patterson. Soon after departing the airport, Dowell felt unwell, travel sickness no doubt, and asked the cabbie to pull over. Unable safely to continue, a decision was taken to have the taxi head back to Bristol where a hotel for the night was eventually found and the journey home completed by train on the Sunday morning.

One irony of the whole episode, of course, is that a repeat of it was avoided only three weeks later. On 21 April, we were away to Colchester United and, unsurprisingly given its relative proximity to Stansted airport, quite a few victims of the Bristol scandal, myself included, were already booked to fly with *Easyjet*. I suspect a few people kept to their word of boycotting the airline thereafter but we set off to Ponteland airport with some trepidation at the usual ungodly hour.

As you may know, there was to be no recurrence of *Easyjet*'s "zero tolerance" policy but, although the outward flight was entirely uneventful as I recall, tension was evident on the flight home. Soon after take-off, the usual drinks trolley appeared but the cabin crew, whilst happy to serve anonymously dressed passengers such as myself, took it upon themselves to refuse service arbitrarily to anyone in a Sunderland shirt or who might otherwise be identified as that most dangerous of creatures, the football spectator.

This scandalous prejudice, as one might expect, provoked complaints but these were greeted merely with the expected response that the question of to whom alcohol would or would not be served was a matter for the discretion of the staff some of whom, for all I know, had been on our flight at Bristol and keen to extract further retribution. I remember that as we left the plane at Ponteland, the usual cordiality and greetings between passengers and staff at the top of the steps were replaced with some hostile exchanges, some of which on our part may have failed the political correctness test. I'm not condoning that or, come to think, maybe I am.

To digress, that game at Colchester, which we lost 3–1, must have been the kick in the backside we needed to push on and secure promotion with the Carlos Edwards inspired victory at home to Burnley, assisted by Derby's defeat at Crystal Palace. It was also remarkable in being without doubt the worst, most decrepit ground I have ever watched us at and I've seen us at close to 100 stadia. The experience was not just unpleasant but tangibly unsafe, apart from not being able to actually see the match. Thank God they've moved to a new ground is all I can say, as how Layer Road had a safety certificate is a complete mystery to anyone in attendance that day.

So, *Easyjet* flight EZ576 wasn't exactly *United 93* and the trek home wasn't the evacuation from the Normandy beaches. It was, however, a unique experience in my more than thirty years of following Sunderland away from home and one in which one realised that it was possible for those who control football clubs and those whose lives revolved around those clubs can, however briefly, come together as one.

We all believe we are fortunate to support our club, as hard as it may be at times. That night, it really felt special to support Sunderland and made that day at Kenilworth Road Luton a few weeks later all the sweeter, when Sunderland collected the Championship trophy.

We probably ought not to have been surprised after the magnanimity of the gesture of the testimonial proceeds being donated to fund child health care in our city and in Ireland, a gesture which has since shamed more and more pampered players, even Mary Poppins up the road, into similar gestures.

The final words on that night belong to Niall himself as told to the *Echo*: "Saturday's journey home from Cardiff was certainly one of the more eventful ones. The situation developed, which led to the cancellation of the flight for the 100 or so loyal supporters. Myself and members of my staff were on board this flight and vehemently oppose the airline's view that there was disruptive behaviour aboard the plane.

The mood was humorous and everyone was in good spirits after our fine victory. Nonetheless, we were faced with a situation where our fans were stranded and needed assistance. The club was happy to arrange transport back to the North East. The group included children, elderly and disabled fans and their safety and wellbeing was paramount. Thankfully, everyone returned home safely and we will now draw a line under this."

Niall Quinn, as modest as ever!

Chapter Six
Gavin Callaghan

A Romantic Risk Amidst Impending Peril: Quinn, Drumaville
and the Irish Economic Crisis

It took four months to move from rhetoric to reality. From an emotional London lunch with former Chairman Sir Bob Murray to Niall Quinn's ordination as the saviour of Sunderland, the Drumaville Consortium set about completing one of football's most romantic risks.

In an era when footballing history is now routinely secondary to fiscal prudency from club owners, the scale of the risk that Quinn took on has never really been fully appreciated.

By the time Quinn donned his black coat and red scarf and left the Stadium of Light for the final time, few can be forgiven for believing that both Wearside and Britain had been in the grip of recession for what seemed an eternity.

That, of course, wasn't the case. Under Quinn's stewardship, Sunderland was to become known (especially on the Emerald Isle) as SundIreland with the foundations of Quinn's footballing house being built on the fortunes of men who had made their money during the economic boom.

Before any of that, Quinn had to plot a strategy for how he could convince his fellow countrymen that his magic carpet ride was not only destined for the Premier League but that it was first, ready to fly.

In the months leading up to the eventual announcement on 3 July 2006 that Drumaville had completed a 90% takeover, Quinn sought the advice of people that knew the game - it's pressures and it's pitfuls, but also people that knew him and his deep affection for Sunderland football club and surrounding region.

One of the people he spoke with was Denis Brosnan - the head of the Kerry Group, whilst at the opening day races of the March 2006 Cheltenham festival. Brosnan had close links to the Irish millionaires J.P. McManus and John Magnier who once had large stakes in Manchester United. Quinn took his advice seriously and later described the experience as an education.

Quinn long had the aspiration to help Sunderland return to the team they were when he was one half of the most deadly striking partnership in the Premier League. But he wasn't a businessman. He knew how football worked but only from the viewpoint that he could put the ball in the back of the net and negotiate a contract for himself every four years. Wage bills, marketing, ticket sales, sponsorship deals and agents fees, were understandably an alien concept to him.

But he left Cheltenham motivated and clear what he had to do to succeed in making sure his bid came to fruition. Later that month he met Bob Murray in London and discussed the idea of the sale. Murray and Quinn's relationship had become fractious after the Irishman had written to Murray denouncing the treatment of Mick McCarthy who had been dismissed from his duties as Sunderland manager that same month. But Murray knew his time was up. He was Red and White through and through and the prospect of being the one who finished off the club he and his city loved was too much.

Newspaper reports suggested that Murray was moved to tears at the lunch as he regaled the club's plight to an even more eager Quinn.

When the meeting ended, Sunderland's former talisman boarded a flight back to Ireland with one mission on his mind; find investors and find them quickly.

With Quinn as popular in Ireland as any living (or dead) Irish footballer is ever likely to be, he knew he wouldn't be short of a few people willing to hear him out. Quickly word spread he was looking for businessman with money to spare who might fancy the challenge. He sounded out potential investors in a way that became commonplace over the next six years; the racecourse.

Quinn's new fantasy football team that was destined for the Stadium of Light boardroom, consisted of himself and eight other Irish businessmen who had made their fortunes the hard way.

In other words, they were men who understood the psychology of sport and especially the football fan having been the financial beneficiaries in their own individual businesses, of ordinary hardworking men and women.

Having owned and ran successful pubs, travel companies, property businesses and hotels, it was considered by Quinn that the Consortium had the right mix of people with a thorough enough understanding of 'punters' and of football itself.

Thus the Drumaville Consortium was born.

The total cost of the takeover was reported to be in the region of £18.4 million which in today's terms, is relatively modest. However, after a previous decade that had seen a 50,000 all-seater stadium and world-class training facilities built, the club's finances were precarious.

Such facts made Quinn's gamble all the more unlikely to succeed. Yes he was supported by eight successful businessman but with the increasingly gloomy oratory from across the Atlantic about sub-prime mortgages, the Irish banking fraternity's love affair with property development coming to an abrupt end and talk of globalisations' first financial test looming large on the horizon, Quinn and his investors could ill afford to be complacent.

In other words, Quinn's urgency to move Sunderland from a club owned by an Irish consortium to a club owned by an Irish-American billionaire, may well have been the wisest move he ever made.

Having not experienced a recession since the 1980s, the Irish economy was considered one of the strongest in the Eurozone. In fact, whilst Britain was recovering from John Major's Black Wednesday catastrophe, the Irish economy was set to embark on what became known as the Celtic Tiger years, spanning from 1994 to 2007.

With a low corporate tax rate, weak banking regulation and a financial management system that was in its infancy and therefore open to exploitation from shrewd businesses, the expansion of credit lending was both inevitable and commonplace in Ireland. The result was that between 2004 and 2008, Ireland's debt to foreign banks, rose from an estimated 15 billion euro to 110 billion euro.

Alarmingly for Sunderland AFC and Niall Quinn, many of the problems encountered by the Irish banks stemmed from too close a relationship to the Irish property market which was totally unsustainable. With almost half of the Drumaville Consortium's membership dependent upon the Irish property market for their millions, Sunderland couldn't take chances.

How different the Sunderland story might have been had Carlos Edwards not rattled in that screamer against Burnley on the cold Friday night at the Stadium of Light that all but guaranteed an improbable promotion to the sporting financial capital of the world. Because for Drumaville, they knew their foray into football was a short-term venture but one that had devastating long term consequences if they didn't exercise the same canny opportunism that had made them their millions.

By the time of their first anniversary at the club, the Irish economy was showing its first real signs of an impending recession. A reality backed up by Government finances that were missing their targets and losing millions in missing taxes. By the end of the Consortium's second season and with survival in the Premier League confirmed, Ireland's economic bubble burst and recession on the Emerald Isle was confirmed.

And the news for Sunderland's Consortium continued to get worse. A recession was soon to become a depression. Contractions of as high as 14% in one financial year were forecast and then matched. In the first financial quarter of 2009 alone - around the Easter of Drumaville's third season in charge - Ireland's economy had contracted by 8.7%.

The Irish unemployment rate was rising steadily from 4.2% in 2007 meaning that with less disposable income, people were unable to spend money in pubs, property or on hotels in anywhere near the same way they had been doing during the Celtic Tiger years.

The result was the residential and commercial property markets collapsed with businesses being declared bankrupt and millionaires losing everything seemingly overnight. What's more, it was estimated that almost 35,000 people emigrated from Ireland in 2009 as a result of the depression.

Lost income, lost spending, lost profit and an economy that had lost international credibility, meant that 2009 was a bad year to be an Irish businessman.

What was more, Sunderland were intertwined with the Anglo-Irish bank having arranged a debenture mortgage with the institution in May 2007. In fairness to Quinn, this was in the same year that Anglo-Irish was awarded the 'Bank of the year" award. How foolish that looked 12 months later.

What did this mean for Sunderland fans? Well in essence, a football club reliant upon Irish money was about as appealing as Howard Wilkinson becoming Black Cats manager in 2003.

What was eminently clear for Quinn was that if he didn't find an investor from outside of Ireland, his magic carpet would have barely made the runway but more probably, would be facing the kind of downward fiscal spiral that Leeds, Charlton and Southampton fans have had to endure in recent years.

Fortunately for Sunderland fans, whilst we were deliriously celebrating Kieran Richardson's winner against Newcastle at the Stadium of Light in October 2008 or Mike Ashley's mishandling of the club up the road that led to their 2009 relegation, our Chairman was far busier making sure Tyneside's misery wasn't repeated down the road on Wearside.

That summer, he had met with Irish-American billionaire Ellis Short. Short had made his money in private equity in Texas but had agreed to meet with Quinn and discuss a possible investment in the club.

Indeed, by the time Shay Given bent down to pick the ball out of his net for the second time on that Saturday afternoon, Quinn had already moved a giant stride closer to allaying his Irish fears.

By the summer of 2008, conventional wisdom would have suggested that any Chairman looking for a buyer might have boarded a flight to Russia or the Gulf. But it was Texas and a billionaire with Irish roots that would be sourced as a potential financier of SundIreland.

In the mire of numbers and talk of economic recessions and depressions it is easy to forget that the figurehead for Sunderland - the man who fans were pinning their hopes on and who the unforgiving media were watching with a hawkeye for the slightest slip - was simply a former footballer. And to be more precise, a former footballer who also used to drink and gamble as Quinn candidly admits in his autobiography.

How then did Niall Quinn manage to steer a consortium of hardy and streetwise millionaires into buying an ailing football club steeped in debt and rooted to the foot of the second tier of English football? And after that, convince an American billionaire that whilst the world's financial centre was about to fall from under it, it would be a good idea to invest tens of millions of pounds into a football club that's most recent achievement was to be known nationally as the whipping boys?

As Louis Fitzgerald from the Drumaville Consortium told the *Irish Independent* in 2012... "Quinn had the magic touch".

Magic touch? Yes. None of us who know what Niall Quinn did for Sunderland would describe his antics over the his six years in charge as anything other than magic. But if he was blessed with majesty from birth, the risk he took in buying Sunderland was also beginning to bear tangible results - something that is key in attracting the eye of any investor.

Promotion and survival aside, SundIreland was becoming a brand and whilst some clubs might be foolish enough to believe that everyone in the United States, Canada, Australia or China has heard of you, Quinn injected realism into Sunderland's marketing ventures. Ireland was practical and realistic. Irish investors, an Irish Chairman, for a spell, an Irish manager, plenty of Irish players and now an Irish fanbase that looks as though it will outlive Quinn, Drumaville and certainly Roy Keane.

To this day, Sunderland is the only club to be owned by a major Irish investor. Gone are the days of J.P. McManus and Manchester United's close association with their friends across the sea.

And whilst talk of a green and white striped away kit proved to be little more than hyperbole, Ireland's obsession with the North East's largest city was growing.

Ahead of the 2007–2008 premier league season, Aer Arann announced a new flight path from Dublin to Newcastle which would see the ferrying of a new generation of Black Cats' fans to and from the Stadium of Light.

The result for the local economy was an increase in hotel bookings, restaurant footfall and pubs packed out on matchdays with what became affectionately known as "the Irish lads".

There was talk that in 2007, a year after the consortium had bought the club and a year before recession struck Ireland, that investors from the Republic were keen to buy land and build on Wearside.

And as the rumour mill began to swirl over whether or not Guinness would be unveiled as the new shirt sponsor, Quinn secured the shirt services of one of Ireland's largest independent bookmakers in Boylesports to the tune of £15 million. Boylesports was also the first shirt sponsor to appear on the famous red and white Sunderland shirt after Reg Vardy - a famous and integral local motor dealers in Sunderland, signalling the arrival of a new dawn on Wearside.

As an investor being shown around the club or more specifically, as an Irish investor being shown around the club, everywhere you looked the place had an air of the green, white and gold.

This hadn't happened by chance, but by choice.

And just had Quinn had planned all along, it was enough to convince Ellis Short to become the sole owner of Sunderland football club, a year after initially buying a 30 per cent stake.

The Drumaville Consortium went into Sunderland as one and they left as one. On their terms, having masterminded one of the most improbable football club purchases and stewardship in the modern game.

It is estimated that the Consortium ploughed over £50 million into the club in under three years. Investment against the backdrop of looming fiscal peril - not just in the country they lived and loved by the very industries they called their own.

In essence, against their accountant's better judgment, Drumaville's investors risked millions on the say so of Quinn.

Their commitment to Quinn and his Sunderland project, is evidence of what can happen when football clubs are run by people that are passionate about the power of the club to change a city and inspire its people.

Reports suggest the investors departed Wearside with a loss of £15million. Quinn challenges this suggestion and is adamant each member of the Consortium made a profit. Either way, had it not been for a giant touch of magic from the 6ft 6in Irishman Quinn and his ability to persuade "the American fella" as he was known, to come on board, the losses could and almost certainly would have been far worse.

Sunderland as a club has deployed all three modules of economic prototypes in the last decade, the good, the bad and the damn right risky. Quinn, in some way or another, has been at the club to experience them all.

Bob Murray's economic plan was simply try and compete and at all costs. It meant Sunderland were financially finished despite Mick McCarthy's heroics in achieving promotion with a squad that was barely good enough to finish mid-table in the Championship in any other year.

Under Quinn, it was the politics of chance. Economists and business-man will preach that no venture is 100% certain and that each carries risks. Quinn will assert that as someone to whom Sunderland "Got under my skin", the opportunity to save his club when they were floundering on the brink of bankruptcy was too good to miss. The reality, however, was that Quinn was playing poker without even looking at his cards.

Looking back, we are glad that he did it. Grateful he saved us and that there is a new, brighter future to look forward to on Wearside, but perhaps unknowing of just how risky this particular game of football really was.

Some might characterise life in the boardroom before Short as a kind of 'back- of-an-envelope-see-how-it-goes' organisation. Perhaps that is unfair to Quinn who grew in stature and influence in boardroom circles as his time at the top went on, even appearing before the prestigious Culture, Media and Sport select committee in parliament to give evidence on football governance.

The risk that Drumaville and Quinn took in spending close to £100 million on transfers in their time together, despite the Irish economy going bust, is surprising in that the consortium existed of such successful busi-nessmen. But unsurprising in as much as those same businessmen, like the tens of thousands of Black Cats around the world, the wider football family and the watching media, were mesmerised by the romance of Quinn's unbelievable story as a footballer, Sunderland fan and now Chairman.

Under the American, it is a smoother, slicker operation that is equipped to take on the mighty challenges of top flight English football free from the fear of the daily news bulletins on RTE.

How long for is still unknown. Short's love-affair may well end the minute Sunderland return to the top 10 and he sees the chance to recoup his losses. The end result might be the kind of foreign ownership that modern football fans dread and dream of in equal measure. Quinn's work may have been for nothing.

The truth is, it is in the nature of the beast. Stints of romanticism in the beautiful game are, for anyone outside the traditional top four clubs, short-lived and precious.

What is for certain is that Niall Quinn was the chief architect of Sunderland's latest glorious chapter. It was a chapter, which defied the odds and proved that the Irishman was as creative in the boardroom, as he was in the penalty box.

The scale of the stakes in Quinn and Drumaville's giant game of poker may not have been evidently clear to the thousands that poured into the Stadium of Light week after week but when the sober eye of history begins to judge his time at the top, the record will show that Quinn masterminded the most romantic risk in modern English football and he did it the eye of an almighty storm.

Chapter Seven
Temporary Gamble
– Chris Siddell

It is mid to late 2008, the winter clouds are gathering over land, the North Sea down at Roker is beginning to froth up at the sides of the pier, the winter chill is on its way and the Stadium of Light corridors are no exception to this…a frosty undertone beginning to force cracks in the club's foundations, as a new wind of change bursts through Wearside.

There could be no doubting that by this point the magic carpet ride was well and truly underway and in full flight. As supporters, we had already experienced Niall Quinn's promise of never a dull moment. There was his disastrous spell as manager, the appointment of Roy Keane, followed by promotion to the Premier League and subsequent survival. Then came the Ellis Short investment as the Drumaville boys started struggling to provide funding for investment in the club. However, just as the arrival of billionaire Short seemed to secure the future and stability of the club, the carpet sojourn started to stutter, and things took a turn for the worse.

The relationship Quinn had with manager Roy Keane was key to our success as a club on and off the field under the former Manchester United captain's rein, yet the pressure of the Premier League along with the arrival of Texan Ellis Short began to put a strain on this unorthodox bond between the two Irishmen.

Under the Drumaville boys things were simple for Keane. The Irish consortium was far from hands on when it came to how Quinn and Keane ran the football side of things. They left the football to the professionals who had made a career out of the game and Quinn handled Keane to perfection.

He knew all too well from his playing days with the Republic of Ireland that Keane could be incredibly volatile, and equally as stubborn when he wanted to be, the most public display of this being the 2002 World Cup saga, in which Roy Keane, then captain of Ireland flew home from the Japan/

South Korea tournament, following a fall out with then Republic manager – Mick McCarthy. That all ended with Quinn having to sit in front of a packed press room and explain the disappearance of Roy Keane and with Quinn's admission from his autobiography that he was fully in support of McCarthy in this most public of spats, it was definitely something Quinn was keen to avoid this time round.

It took all of Quinn's people skills to accommodate Keane and allow him the space he needed to lead the squad, whilst still retaining control over him. Keane wasn't subject to boardroom demands or strict instructions, but instead he received suggestions and encouragement when it was needed. It worked. Suddenly the people of Sunderland realised they were onto a good thing. Quinn had managed to tame Keane and had showed the maturity and skill of a chairman with far more experience in the job.

The work Quinn had been doing at the club was astonishing. He had managed to take a club that was really struggling to hold on to frustrated supporters, never mind perform on the field, and turn things around. His honesty, bold decisions (like the one to appoint Keane in the first place), and willingness to talk to the supporters in both the press and in person, made him a very popular chairman. The club was once again becoming 'our' club. A club we could relate to and a club we wanted to be a part of once again.

Within just a couple of years, we had been catapulted from the bottom of the Championship into the Premier League, and then survived with a couple of games to spare. In the Summer of 2008 things were looking good for Sunderland. But as the new season got underway things started to get very difficult for Quinn as chairman.

The team did not start fantastically well on the field. By the end of September Keane's side had managed just two wins from six Premier League games, and had barely scraped into the fourth round of the League Cup, twice failing to beat lower league opposition in normal time. The poor results were compounded by the fact Keane had spent a whole lot of money over the summer. The players he brought in cost the club somewhere around £25 million pounds, and the man who had put that money forward wanted to know why it wasn't working.

Ellis Short's arrival at the club will no doubt be the greatest legacy that Quinn will leave the club in the long term. The American billionaire continues to provide the club with an incredibly strong business brain, and of course, financial stability. Short had taken a 30% stake of the Drumaville Consortium that season, giving him the largest stake, and effectively, control of the club. Indeed, Niall Quinn said at the beginning of 2009 to the *Sunderland Echo* that "Ellis Short is vital, but because he doesn't like publicity, Sunderland fans weren't aware how important he is."

Short might have taken up Irish Citizenship, but he is an American at heart, and as such Roy Keane was just another employee, not a national hero. He dared to do what the Drumaville boys had chosen to avoid. He questioned Keane. He wanted to know what was going on, and he wanted to know why. Why had his 25 million pound investment brought just two wins from six, and what could be done to turn things around?

Keane did not like that.

Ellis Short was not the only one asking questions, the entire stadium was now asking questions. Just days before Short was officially announced as a shareholder, Sunderland faced Northampton Town in the third round of the League Cup at home. Anyone who was there will remember that night, despite trying their best to forget it.

It was awful. The team played badly, and worse still, they seemed to be playing with no commitment. Two last gasp goals from Anthony Stokes saved the team from defeat and winning the penalty shootout lottery saw us into the next round, but the damage was done. The cracks really started to show in Keane's temperament, and he had a go at the fans. It was at this game, that stories emerged of Keane performing a Kung-Fu kick on a flip-chart inside the home dressing room, confronting players and alledgedly informing them they would never play for Sunderland again...the pressure was showing.

The man who had to deal with all of this was of course Quinn. He had a massive investor asking questions, a set of supporters who deserved better and a manager who could explode at any minute. For many people that would have been too much, but not Quinn. For two months he held everything together, and we even managed a couple of positive results (including beating local rivals Newcastle United), but eventually, Keane went AWOL following a 4–1 home defeat at the hands of Bolton Wanderers.

Knowing all too well how Keane can react when he is backed into a corner (see the Irish World Cup debacle in 2002), Quinn did everything he could to shield the Sunderland manager from the owner and the fans alike, but it was still too much for Keane to handle. Short wanted to have his manager available to speak with whenever he wanted, he wanted things to be done his way, he wanted the club to be run like a business, there were signs Keane was not up for that.

There was no choice really, and Quinn knew it. Short was, and is, the future of the club. Keane was just a young, temperamental manager. When it came down to it there was only one man he could afford to upset, and that was Keane. The changes in the way things were done around the club were always going to have an impact on the manager, and Quinn did all he could to make the impact as small as possible for Keane.

Questions about the commitment of Keane and the way he managed the squad surfaced, and there was little Quinn could do to defend Keane. The manager had never moved to the region, and would often not be present at training. For Short, that was not good enough, that was not how you ran a business. The man in charge of the team was expected to be the first to arrive and the last to leave, not just turn up when he felt like travelling.

To go with all the questions about his commitment; his management style and people skills were also being called into question. The players were living in fear of Keane. They did not seem to be enjoying life as footballers and it was showing on the field. The squad needed to adapt, to change, and Quinn had to communicate that to Keane.

With another manager it might have turned out fantastically well, but not with Keane. What he had achieved was amazing, taking a club from the bottom of the Championship to the Premier League in such a short time. But the pressure of the Premier League was too much, and no matter how much Quinn tried to shield him and help him, it was just not enough.

Keane never really grasped that things needed to change. He never accepted that, effectively, he had a new boss in Ellis Short, and the new boss wanted things to change. Quinn knew this and tried to bring about the change slowly and subtly, but Keane was having none of it.

It all came to a head after the home game with Bolton on 29 November 2008. The preparation for that match had been a disaster. Having lost the previous Sunday to West Ham, rumours were flying around that the training ground had been empty most of the week after a combination of rest days and Christmas parties. Not the way it should be for a struggling team. Despite going ahead after ten minutes, the match was even more of a disaster.

Bolton were a team that we should have been beating, they had made a good start, but Sunderland were at home and this was a game the club will have targeted as a victory. Instead they were humiliated 4–1 in a game that saw many fans leave well before the full time whistle and those left behind made it clear what they thought of the performance. Stupid mistakes had cost Keane's men badly, and although the home side did create some chances, it could well have been more than four for the visitors.

After the match things did not seem too bad for Keane. Unlike the game against Northampton he did not talk about the abuse from the crowd, he did not tell everyone it was the worst day of his career, instead he was surprisingly upbeat. He spoke about how it was individual mistakes that had cost the team, that we needed to bounce back from it. Although not perfect words, they did not give any indication of what was about to happen.

Questions were asked, and enough was enough, things needed to change now. It was time for Keane to admit that it may have been his management that was causing some of the problems, and that maybe a new approach would be better. Keane was not a man that was going to admit that.

Instead he went AWOL. He just disappeared and ultimately never returned. The week that followed the match against Bolton seemed to last an eternity. The whole of Sunderland just waiting for news on what was going on, all eyes again were on our chairman. What would he do, how could he solve this one?

Knowing that relegation was a real possibility, Quinn knew the squad needed to be led by a manager who could get the best out of the players. Keane could have, and possibly should have been that man, he had proved that in the past two seasons. Quinn did everything he could to talk Keane around, to talk some sense into him and persuade him to change his mind, and his methods. He worked tirelessly and stealthily to avoid the media, who, as ever, were looking for a big story.

Quinn was not going to give them that story though. He wasn't going to make a big scene or have a public slagging match. Eventually there was nothing more that Quinn could do to make Keane change. Keane was adamant that he was going to resign, and Quinn knew that accepting the resignation was the only thing he could do.

Every manager faces difficulty in their career, and it is those difficult times that make people into great managers. Those winter months in 2008-2009, if he had guided us through them, could have made Keane into a great manager. Instead, they effectively ended his Premier League career. We will never know how it would have turned out.

Instead Quinn found himself in an uncomfortably familiar position. Just like he had in 2002, the big man was sitting in front of the press explaining that Roy Keane had left. Quinn once again proved himself to be the perfect gentleman that day. Refusing to blame Keane and standing up for him in front of the watching press was hugely admirable. The tabloids wanted a story, they wanted to hear about how Keane had exploded and burnt all his bridges, but Quinn, despite all that had happened, never lowered himself to that level.

Going onto that press conference was possibly the bravest thing Quinn had ever done, certainly as our chairman. Where most clubs would have sent out a spokesman, or circulated a press release, Quinn stepped up and faced the press in person. But that was not the end of his bravery. The decisions he had to make after that press conference may well have been the most difficult, and certainly the most important of his time as chairman. He had to keep us up.

Quinn had to take a temporary gamble.

Sunderland, up to this point, was pretty much the definition of a yo-yo club. It was something we were accustomed to. A year or so in the top flight, relegation, and then promotion back within a couple of years. The main focus of Quinn, and Ellis Short, was to put a stop to that and establish

Sunderland firmly in the Premier League. The decision Quinn was about to make would play a huge part in doing that. Relegation at this point would have been a disaster for the club, on and off the field. Quinn had to get this right.

The first thing Quinn needed to do was to get the team ready for a huge game at Old Trafford. It had taken four days to try and clear the air with Keane, and all of a sudden it was Thursday. Ricky Sbragia was appointed as caretaker manager with no real time to do anything before the game at in Manchester. I'm sure inside he knew Keane would probably not return, but he couldn't act or make any decisions until it was official.

Sbragia had arrived at Sunderland as a first team coach under Keane, but knew Sunderland very well after a long spell as reserve team coach in the nineties. He had worked under Sir Alex Ferguson at Manchester United, and had also been involved at Bolton. But ultimately he had no experience at all in management at a senior level, with his background firmly in reserve teams, coaching and scouting. Everyone knew he was not the man for the job, he couldn't be, Sbragia was just a caretaker until a new manager could be found surely?

At least that's what the whole of Sunderland *thought* they knew.

Finding and appointing the right manager is incredibly difficult and stressful at the best of times, but appointing one half way through the season, when you're in the relegation zone. That makes things that little bit harder. With Christmas on the way, Quinn got to work searching for his man.

Having seen Quinn convince Keane to come to the club when we sat at the bottom of the Championship the whole of Sunderland was incredibly optimistic about the search, everyone touting a new big name replacement for Keane. In reality that was never going to happen, not at this point. It was far too big of a risk, and Quinn knew that. Appointing a big name, Premier League manager would require big Premier League money. That was too big of a risk for Quinn and Short.

A big name manager is great, but it does not guarantee Premier League survival, and from the position we were in, relegation was a real possibility. It would take a long term contract and some serious wages to attract a manager from another club. No Premier League manager would be willing to leave a stable club and join up with one in turmoil, and any manager at a club also in trouble was not someone the club wanted!

Even managers in the Championship were not particularly willing to join up. The better managers backed themselves to bring their own team up into the Premier League rather than keep Sunderland safe. Quinn knew that getting one of these managers would have meant putting the club in a financially unsettling position and he wasn't going to do that.

Then there were those who didn't have a job. There were plenty of unemployed managers with Premier League experience around. Alan Curbishley being the main name that was mentioned. The big problem Quinn faced with these guys was once again money and contracts. Of course many of them would have been happy to take over, but they wanted security. They wanted the same long term contracts with Premier League money, regardless of what happened.

Had the new manager; say Curbishley for arguments sake, took over on a long contract with Premier League money, things could have gone horribly wrong for the club. Had we been relegated, the new manager would have been free from blame. 'It wasn't his squad, he did all he could, but it was an impossible task' is how the papers would have read. Then we would be a Championship team paying the manager Premier League money, without the funds to buy out his contract and sack him if he was useless.

Going down that route would have been a huge risk for the long term stability of the club, and Quinn knew that. The appointment of any new manager is always going to include an element of risk. The job of a good chairman is to minimise that risk and Quinn just couldn't risk bringing in someone completely new on big money.

All too often in football, even the most experienced of chairmen make big mistakes when appointing a manager, and many struggle to see the wood for the trees when searching for their man. Not Quinn though. During his time searching for a new manager, he noticed something fantastic was happening at the Academy of Light. He noticed things were changing.

Sbragia had taken over a squad which was completely demoralised and ready to cave in on itself. The general consensus was that if a new and experienced manager was not in place quickly, then it would do just that. But what Sbragia achieved was incredible, and some might even say a miracle. He took that squad, and almost instantly, he turned things around.

With barely a day to prepare, Sbragia's first test was a visit to Old Trafford. Nobody expected anything less than a big defeat, but we came away with our heads held high, United winning 1–0 after an injury time winner. Surely it was just a fluke, one of those strange anomalies in football that saw a team in tatters almost overcome the giant. Quinn started to take notice though, when a week later West Bromwich visited the Stadium of Light. Still without a permanent manager, we were three goals to the good at half time. After Djibril Cisse added another from the spot the game ended 4–0... to Sunderland!

Another week went by and still without a manager it happened again, this time away at Hull. The lads came home with another three points and another four goals, this time winning 4–1. By Boxing Day, three weeks after being appointed Sbragia had racked up seven points in just four games (the Boxing Day fixture with Blackburn was a 0–0 draw). The only blip was a defeat away at Manchester United, a game that saw us lose in injury time.

On 27 December, Quinn took the bold step of appointing Sbragia as the permanent manager. He was given an 18-month contract and just five months to keep the club in the Premier League. Hardly a long term appointment, and certainly a big risk for Quinn and the club. The appointment was a gamble, it was a temporary gamble as it transpired.

Although the results played their part, they were not the reason that Sbragia was appointed. Quinn certainly did not make a knee-jerk reaction to a couple of good results. What he did do was observe what was happening in and around the squad. The players were starting to arrive at, and leave training with a smile on their face. It was one of the things that Keane felt was 'wrong' once Short had arrived, the players were there to train, not to smile in his eyes. But Sbragia was managing to do both, he was training hard with the players, but he was doing it in a way that made them smile. For the first time during 2008 the squad seemed happy.

Under Keane the players had lost their desire. They were living in fear of the manager and didn't have the motivation or desire to play, or even train hard for him. By the time Keane had left, he had drained the squad mentally.

Sbragia knew the players well, and used this to manage them in a completely different way. He was positive, friendly and most importantly, understanding of the players and the situation they were in. Keane could never understand why players were not as good as he was, it was never good enough. But Sbragia changed that, all he wanted was maximum effort from the squad.

The turnaround in those few games Sbragia had as caretaker was astonishing, and the importance of it was not lost on Quinn. He realised that Sbragia had a huge positive effect on the squad, and that even without any experience as a manager; he was a relatively safe bet. Quinn had checked the odds on every option available, and he was certain that the safest bet for Sunderland was not necessarily the top jockey with the shortest odds, but the outsider who knew the course.

I don't think anyone really wanted Sbragia to get the job, even Sbragia himself didn't seem to want it, but Quinn knew that he had to have it, and convinced the Scotsman. The task facing him was huge. Saving the club from relegation was something that seemed impossible, yet it had to be done.

The attitude changed immensely in the squad. The team was not necessarily playing any better, but they were playing with more heart. They were playing for the manager, and it showed.

Perhaps the finest example was at Bolton away. With only a few games left a defeat that day would have destroyed morale and could well have seen us relegated. Bolton at home was of course the last game under Roy Keane. A game that saw the team effectively throw in the towel, succumbing to a 4–1 defeat. This time though, there would be no surrender.

The team fought for every second of the match, and spurred on by an incredible away support, they battled out a 0–0 draw. Sunderland had lost the previous two games and were in serious danger and needed something from the game, in the end a point was enough. Not a great result on paper, but a few months earlier, things would have been very different. This time the team didn't roll over, they didn't give up, and they fought hard for that point. Many fans realised that we might not be the best of teams, but we did have the heart to stay up.

It happened more than once; Sunderland had games against Tottenham, Arsenal and Fulham where we earned points through determination and desire as oppose to necessarily being better than our opponents. It was not always pretty, but it turned out to be exactly what we needed.

Add to the mix, the fact that all three north-east clubs were vying for survival, with Middlesbrough ensconced in the relegation mire already, Sunderland, Newcastle and Hull City were battling to avoid the last relegation spot in the ultimate battle of the near neighbours.

The last day of the season rolled around and we were still in serious danger. It was a tough day, almost unbearable. Up against Chelsea we knew our chances of getting anything were slim, but those around us had just as daunting fixtures. On the day the team threw everything at it, but Chelsea were just too good. Sunderland lost that day, but so did everyone else, we were safe and the gamble had paid off, cue wild celebrations that day at the SOL, when relegation of Newcastle was confirmed.

Sbragia resigned as manager immediately after we were safe in the Premier League, and the gratitude of Quinn was clear to see. He offered Sbragia a job for life at the club, and once again made all the right moves in front of the camera. Quinn said after the game, "It has been an incredibly emotional day. I haven't had too many days like this in my life, I can tell you. There was a lot of tension, a lot of relief and a little bit of sadness because Ricky Sbragia had decided not to take up the final year of his contract."

This time though, his real genius had been behind the camera. Quinn had not taken the easy way out spending money on a big name manager, but instead made the choice best for the club. Whatever he did was always going to be a gamble, but Quinn had narrowed down the odds and made a temporary gamble that he was certain would pay-off.

He was right, only just, but he was right, but perhaps the biggest gamble of all was to come in the appointment of Steve Bruce, a football man, but with clear Geordie roots.

Chapter Eight
Enter Bruce

Gary Johnson

Following Ricky Sbragia's resignation as Sunderland manager, Niall Quinn admitted the appointment of the 52-year-old as being a "huge gamble", in a very open interview in the *Guardian* in June 2009.

Quinn continues: "We took a gamble on Ricky and it's gone our way. We won the horse race by a photo finish. I have a gambling instinct in me, I always felt Ricky would lift us out of trouble – and he did."

Quinn handed the Scot an 18-month contract to bring back some stability until the end of the season. In what turned out to be a season many of us will never forget, maybe for different reasons, with us just avoiding relegation on the final day, Sbragia achieved his objective by staying out of the bottom three. Sunderland lost 3–2 at the hands of Chelsea at the Stadium of Light, as news filtered that Newcastle and Middlesbrough had lost their Premiership status all was forgotten about another dreadful season.

Everyone was on cloud nine and on this remarkable day in May 2009, except one man. The resignation of Ricky Sbragia as the Sunderland manager left Niall Quinn with yet another difficult position in the search for another manager inside the space of only six months. It was a strange feeling for Sunderland fans as the majority were relieved and excited to have survived a relegation battle over our two bitterest rivals on the last day, but also sad to hear that Sbragia was going to walk away from being the manager of Sunderland Association Football Club.

It was more than a possibility that Sbragia knew that Quinn had secured the Texan takeover in the form of Ellis Short in their appearance on cameras immediately after the Chelsea defeat. There was gratitude and relief pouring out of Quinny's heart in this interview as he thanked Ricky for doing what he was asked to do, save the club from another heart-breaking relegation stain on our history.

Sbragia told Sky Sports after the game: "I do feel that the club needs a bigger name. I took over in a difficult situation. I was asked to keep the club up and I achieved that. I could've been selfish and stayed on but I felt it was best for the club for me to step down."

Sunderland fans were now used to hearing cryptic messages, from when Niall took over the club, to announcing the Drumaville Consortium being part of the finances of the club moving forward, to this "bigger name" that Ricky mentions in his on-air conversations to millions of fans around the world.

Who would Niall turn to next to ensure these relegation battles were never witnessed again and mid table security was the main target under a new manager and different approach under Ellis Short? It was a very important time in the history of Sunderland AFC as Niall Quinn secured a tremendous coup by appointing Ellis Short after meeting him on a round of golf in America. This was the time that every single Sunderland fan dreamed of. A multi-billionaire owner, a Chairman with the passion and dedication and honesty of Niall Quinn, all that was now missing from the perfect formula was a manager who can drive his team up into the top half of the English Premier league.

Niall had to make the correct decision and ensure that the club he grew to adopt through his own playing career would continue to move in the correct direction under his guidance as Chairman. The shortlist seemed to be exactly what it said, short and the manager he targeted as soon as Sbragia left was done with the correct intentions. Quinny knew the area and what it meant to the supporters to have a manager they could put all of their faith and belief into so the new management style could be accepted from the first moment he walked through the Stadium of Light gates in the summer of 2009.

The man who was selected to lead the club into mid-table security was Steve Bruce, an experienced manager who knew the area and understood the expectation levels of the Wearside fans. Niall Quinn admitted that Ricky Sbragia was "a big gamble" but this appointment was also of the same stature with Bruce being a born and bred Newcastle United fan.

Sky Sports News presenter David Craig, who has very close ties with the club and has had a friendship with Niall for over 30 years gave his thoughts on the appointment of Bruce by saying: "Steve and Niall had a very strong and solid relationship, they were very close and Niall had his sights set on getting him after Ricky left the club after survival was confirmed. Bruce really cared about the club and he was all about winning games of football, which maybe came from his Manchester United days and mentality. Niall wanted to show Bruce that he could be manager of this club and go places that Wigan Athletic could not achieve."

Mark Douglas, journalist from *The Journal* speaks about how the Quinn and Steve Bruce relationship formed at the start: "The problem was that Bruce was already in employment and Quinn, a man of principle and integrity, did not intend to disrupt Wigan's season or sully Sunderland's reputation by forcing Bruce to walk out on a chairman who had been good to him.

"The fact that the job was, in essence, kept open for him to take over six months later set firm foundations for a relationship that was built on trust and a mutual understanding. Bruce liked Quinn and the feeling was mutual: they had played football in the same era and both believed that when a man said something, it was up to him to keep his word."

A big deciding factor in the appointment of Steve Bruce, who had finished the 2008–09 season with Wigan Athletic in a lofty 11th placed position, was the availability of funds from the new owner Ellis Short and the freedom to try and attract a different calibre of player under his style. Bruce famously quoted that the difference between managing Wigan with Dave Whelan in charge and joining Sunderland was remarkable by telling the *Daily Mail*: "I haven't had a conversation about how much money there is available, but I have spoken to the owner and he doesn't want to be involved at the bottom [of the Premier League] again. He did say he would back me.

"I have always been good value for money in the transfer market, and I will always try to be. But I'm looking at players I have never looked at before.

"It's like shopping in Harrods now, not Tesco. I don't have specific targets just yet, but I do have one or two ideas up my sleeve."

The theme of location and Steve Bruce's past roots and allegiances through his Sunderland managerial career will run through this chapter in almost every shape and form. Niall made the decision when Steve was on holiday in Portugal with his family and was told by his Father, Joe, in his own words: "To fill your boots, son!" Bruce was initially rejected by Sunderland in the late 1970's when he failed to get noticed as a young centre-half, but this opportunity was one that he simply could not refuse. Sunderland had become fragile and lacked a cutting edge with previous managers and this was something Niall identified when he recruited Bruce on a three-year contract. Quinn spoke to *The Independent* at the time and said: "We have been brittle at times, what we want is a Sunderland team that is determined, tough, that represents the Steve Bruce philosophy."

Sunderland fans, at the time, believed that Niall Quinn had made the perfect appointment with Bruce. Obviously, some had reservations about his childhood love of Newcastle, but Bruce admitted that he was a professional football manager and where he came from had no influence on the way he wanted to perform as a manager for Sunderland AFC. Quinn and Short made true their claims that funds would be available for Steve and players started arriving for the start of the 2009–10 season with a new hope floating around the City.

The way Quinn spoke about Bruce in the opening press conference also showed the fans and the media that they were in this together and wanted to share the same dream and vision for the club. Mark Douglas, from *The Journal* remembers the conference vividly: "When he took over, Quinn stood alongside Bruce at his first press conference. They answered questions about Bruce's heritage as if they were singing from the same hymn sheet and, tellingly, the new manager said that the prospect of working under a "proper" football man was a huge draw for him. The implication being that he would get time, for Quinn would have rather sold his soul than sacked a manager."

What everyone in the football circles knew about Steve Bruce was his ability to spot a signing for a great price with players such as Valencia, Rodellaga, and Palicios from abroad to adapt to his style of football and was evident at his former club, Wigan. These players have all become household names in the Premier League and owe a lot to Bruce for his ability to see their early potential and develop it in the best league in the world. Niall Quinn must have also been very aware of this management trait from Bruce and would be excited to see the next crop of his scouting become household names within his Sunderland squad. The link between Sunderland and Manchester United has always been a strong connection, especially after Keane and Sbragia were in charge before him and this bond grew stronger when Bruce signed Fraizer Campbell from Manchester United for a reported £3.5m. Bruce, who won nearly every medal and trophy available for Manchester United, would also fit in nicely into this liasion with Old Trafford, due to the link that Keane had enhanced during his time as manager with Niall.

The first signing to capture people's imagination was the arrival of Lorik Cana for £5 million from Marseille, he would become a player that everyone would remember for his presence in the midfield and his never say die attitude going into tackles and headers. He was exactly the player that Sunderland fans appreciated, an experienced and cultured player that was never afraid of stamping his authority down in a game.

Whilst Bruce was re-shaping the Sunderland team and making his own mark on the squad, he was also selling players for very decent prices. He sold Michael Chopra and Dean Whitehead for a combined fee of £6m and the framework of what Niall Quinn envisaged was becoming a reality with players who never really created much moving on and new players with a hunger and desire were brought in to kick start the club in the right direction. Short provided the money so that other clubs who expressed an interest in the Marseille captain could see that Sunderland would stick around until the deal was concluded. This marked a significant change for Sunderland as attractive players were now choosing to come to Sunderland for the right reasons; the belief was beginning to grow inside the club as well as around the North East.

Bruce also appointed another no-nonsense midfielder, who knows all about the North East and the region's high expectations, with the signing of Lee Cattermole. Cattermole, who formed a relationship at Wigan with Bruce, was his first breakthrough after a long discussion with Dave Whelan was finally won and £6 million was the price agreed by the two clubs. There seemed to be a pattern slightly emerging with young, hungry, British players being identified as what was required to avoid the 'brittle' tag that Quinn had spoken of when Bruce joined in June.

Then on the fifth of that month, Sunderland broke their transfer record as Steve Bruce secured the signature of Darren Bent. This really was the start of something special and for £10 million it was actually a shrewd deal agreed by Short, Quinn and Bruce in order to get the English striker on board. Sunderland had never seen an arrival of such magnitude and for Ipswich, Charlton and Tottenham Hotspur he had played 299 games in all competitions and scored a remarkable 118 goals. Bent left the capital after scoring 17 goals for Spurs after he fell out of favour with then White Hart Lane gaffer Harry Redknapp. Steve Bruce used this breakdown between Bent and Redknapp to his advantage and moved in quickly as soon as he knew he was available. The framework discussed was continuing to get stronger with yet another hungry British player itching to prove a lot of people wrong.

Steve Bruce spoke with pride as he got his man by saying: "Good things come to those who wait. He's everything I want. He has 50 goals in 100 Premier League starts and that speaks volumes about why we are bringing him to the club."

Niall Quinn and Ellis Short must have been delighted with the transfer market activity that Bruce produced in such a short period of time. This buzz that the Darren Bent signing created was something that happened rarely on Wearside.

The buzz continued into Steve Bruce's first game in charge as Bent scored the winner away to Bolton Wanderers at the Reebok Stadium. Sunderland continued to have a strong start to the season and that man Darren Bent kept popping up in the headlines for all the right reasons. The impact that Bent brought to Sunderland was nothing short of phenomenal with him scoring eight times in his opening nine league games. The early form of Bruce lead the team to the heights of seventh in the Premier league and maybe, for once Sunderland AFC were enjoying a moment of good fortune as well as skill.

One result that really stuck out was against Manchester United at Old Trafford on 3 October 2009, as Bruce looked to impress his former manager Sir Alex Ferguson. Bent scored a brilliant long ranged effort and his partner Kenwyne Jones scored what looked like the winner in front of a stunned travelling support. Unfortunately Anton Ferdinand helped out his Brother's team by sticking out a leg in the dying minutes to deny Sunderland a famous victory at the Theatre of Dreams, however a 2–2 draw at the home of the Champions was credible to say the least.

Another game that cannot be forgotten during this rich vein of form, with Bent scoring one of the craziest goals ever to be witnessed at the Stadium of Light was Liverpool's visit to Wearside on 17 October 2009. Sunderland opened the scoring, with the eventual winning goal, early doors in the fifth minute as Bent struck the ball on to an object in front of the disbelieving Pepe Reina. The ball took a wicked deflection off a Liverpool fan's beachball stricken in front of the goalmouth, to deflect into the South Stand net and send the home faithful into ecstacy or maybe hilarity at the situation. Everything seemed to be running exactly the way, if not even better than Quinn could ever have imagined. Sunderland were flying in the league and the fans could not get enough of Bruce's team and in particular how quickly England striker Darren Bent had settled on Wearside. It felt at this point in my lifetime of supporting the lads that Niall Quinn's "Magic carpet ride" was really starting to get out of the turbulence and be directed into a smooth ride for us all to enjoy. Could Bent now go on to emulate such legendary status as Quinn and his strike partner, Kevin Phillips enjoyed a decade before?

However, being a Sunderland fan all my life means that a sudden air pressure drop on the "Magic carpet", complete with oxygen masks and life vests was all but expected as results followed, which saw us drop down the league and restore that sense of fear and trepidation of what may loom ahead, emotions that come with the territory of following the lads in red and white. We were warned by angry Wigan fans on message boards and radio phone in programmes, early in that summer of 2009, that Steve Bruce always suffers from long spells in a season where three points are as hard to find as a needle in a haystack at times. It happened with Birmingham and

Wigan so the signs were there but no-one quite expected a run of an amazing 14 games without a single league victory. This was the first test for Niall and Ellis to see how their man in charge reacted to a change in fortunes.

During this dreadful run, Bent managed to earn us three important draws through his natural goalscoring ability against Portsmouth, Everton and Blackburn but the most worrying performance for the club came against a rampant Chelsea. Steve Bruce watched on in horror as Chelsea scored an all too easy seven goals past a hapless defence and alarm bells with the board and fans were ringing very loudly following this defeat. Steve Bruce was open in his assessment after the game by telling *BBC Sport*: "There's no getting away from it, we have had our backsides well and truly kicked. We've got a lot of players missing defensively and this is a hard enough place to come when you have a full strength side.

"But we couldn't get near them today, it was a procession, and we can only hope that we pick ourselves up, dust ourselves down, and respond."

Bruce wanted a response from his team but unfortunately it took another six games until the next win was registered in the league. At this point we were placed at fourteenth in the table, the lowest we would feature all season, and a big game was required against the same team that ended Roy Keane's management with Sunderland, Bolton Wanderers.

Who else could Bruce turn to? Who else could score the important goals to end this woeful run? Of course, it would be none other than Darren Bent. The former Charlton striker notched a hat-trick to secure a comfortable 4–0 victory to re-assure the fans that he did have the skills to get the season back on track. This performance was much needed and really got the momentum going as Sunderland went on a run of four games without a defeat. These further five points gave the mood around the club a much needed lift and the season ended with Bruce taking us to thirteenth in the league. This was a superb achievement for the club, especially after the 'winter of discontent' that lead to a barren run of a measly five points from a possible 42 available.

Darren Bent unsuprisingly collected the player of the season award after scoring an incredible 25 goals in all competitions and all the fans were looking forward to what he could achieve in the following campaign. No one though could have predicted what would happen next in Darren Bent's relationship with Sunderland.

So how could Niall and Ellis develop the team further under Bruce? What funds were going to be made available? Who could Bruce attract to the club that although they'd had a bad run mid season, still finished in a respectable thirteenth position? Bruce's activities in pre season of the 2010–11 season could have been his downfall due to relying so much on players who were only here on loan. Bruce managed to smash another transfer record by announcing an eye-opening capture of the Ghana striker Asamoah Gyan for £13m after impressing in the World Cup in South Africa in the summer of 2010. Bruce also drafted in Danny Welbeck, kept on the impressive John Mensah in defence and sealed another loan deal for Nedum Onuoha from Manchester City. The Sunderland manager also brought in Belgian keeper, Simon Mignolet, Titus Bramble and Argentine, Marcos Angeleri all for relatively low amounts to bolster his squad for another attack up the Premier league in his second season.

The start of the season began, like the season before, very positively for Sunderland with only one defeat in the opening nine league games. Confidence was high as the long-awaited north-east derby approached and the fans started to feel the tension and nerves that they had badly missed whilst their rivals Newcastle United were in the Championship the previous season. This was a chance for Steve Bruce to lay all of the media reports, fans comments and message board remarks to bed about where his roots truly lied when he took his newly formed squad to the lions den of St. James' Park on Halloween 2010. Sadly, I was there to see the demolition that occurred in front of my horrified eyes, Newcastle really stepped it up on that day and completely embarrassed not only the Sunderland team who in turn embarrassed the whole city of Sunderland after that display. Cracks were beginning to form with the fans who really did not expect that result after seeing such a positive start in the build up to the game. Fans who questioned where Bruce's heart was during this game had thousands of questions to face after the game. David Craig, was there to see his reaction after the 5–1 defeat adding: "I didn't buy into the whole 'he is from Newcastle' talk that many supporters mentioned when things did not go their way. I was there first hand to see how drained and emotional he looked after the 5–1 loss at St. James' Park. That result really hurt him and I don't think he ever recovered from that performance, but it showed that he cared by the reaction he showed me immediately after the game."

The strangest thing about Bruce's period in charge with Sunderland was exactly how much this result lingered in every supporter's thoughts. If we won or drew a game it was hardly mentioned, as soon as a bad performance was witnessed, it was brought up in discussions and within the newspapers. Was this fair? Was the upbringing of the manager always in the background of everyone's thoughts as a get out clause, a scapegoat option?

Sky Sports senior reporter, Graeme Bailey, agreed by adding: "The appointment of Steve Bruce was always a risk given his Tyneside roots, although widely acclaimed there was always somewhat of an under-current at the Stadium of Light and you could always feel that at games."

But even stranger than that, was how we responded to this awful game. Sunderland embarked on a run of eight games unbeaten, including one of the best performances any Sunderland fan can claim to have seen at Stamford Bridge as Bruce's men completely bossed a game against high flyers Chelsea on their own patch. Niall Quinn said at a talk-in event how much this result pleased Ellis Short, he spoke proudly of this performance and how Ellis Short who was staying in a plush hotel in Asia at the time, was warned for his behaviour and more importantly his volume by the hotel when he heard the full-time whistle to announce Sunderland had beaten one of Europe's finest teams on their day in their own back yard. Maybe all was forgotten about the 5–1 drubbing by the enemy?

When the January transfer window opened in January 2011, Sunderland were placed in a healthy sixth position in the league and even went unbeaten in the full month of January, granted through a very late Newcastle equaliser by Gyan in the dying moments of what looked like another defeat to the Magpies. However, it wasn't the impressive run of form that Sunderland encountered as they entered the new year that made all the news, it was the revelation that Darren Bent had immediately handed in his transfer request following the Newcastle game. This effected everyone. The fans could see in his derby day display that his heart and usual finishing prowess was not there and then the bombshell hit home when Sunderland sold our best striker to Aston Villa on 18 January.

Niall Quinn tried to calm down angry fans by telling them via Kildare TV: "We could have tried to stop it but then we heard that he was already down there [in negotiation with Villa] all we could do was fight to get as good as deal as possible. It was really difficult. I wasn't surprised when he put in the transfer request. I had an inkling. Darren is a terrific guy and he's been great for us over and beyond playing football but about two or three weeks ago I knew there was something up with him."

Was Niall Quinn hiding something and using his charm with the fans on an issue that really threw the season into turmoil? Graeme Anderson from the *Sunderland Echo* said: "As ever, the chairman presented a slick and agreeable figure to the media as he explained the club's reasoning behind Bent's departure – you don't keep an unhappy player, especially one who simply wants more money; and the club's plans to replace him – wait until the summer when you can get better value than the panic-buy January sales.

"However, perhaps things weren't quite as seamless as they might have appeared.

Certainly the view from Steve Bruce's office seemed to be that whether Bent was being greedy or not, might it not have been wiser, if morally repugnant, just to bung him the extra cash?"

The usual mid season blip naturally occurred when Bent disappeared along with his goals and Steve Bruce recorded no wins in his next nine games after January. The main positive from January was the arrival of tricky Benin international, Stephane Sessegnon for a great price of £6 million, another great bit of business by Bruce.

The Bent saga rumbled on and stretched the relationship between Steve and Niall but they still appeared in the media to be fully behind one another. They attended a road show of talk-ins, designed to boost next seasons season ticket sales and their relationship appeared very amicable. They even became the first manager and Chairman to appear on a Sunday morning TV show when they openly and honestly spoke about their club to Chris Kamara and Ben Shephard on *Soccer Sunday*. David Craig hosted the Sunderland talk-in events and commented: "I hosted a talk-in event at Rainton

Meadows with Steve Bruce he was very open and honest about his plans with the club. It showed that he bought into Niall's plans and philosophy by attending these talk in shows. I remember he answered all the questions as accurately as he could and even said things just for that audience."

The season rather petered out but we still managed to finish the season in tenth position, something that Bruce would never stop talking about, after he left the club. The next pre-season was going to be crucial, as Sunderland had lost the majority of their loan players; Bent was still not replaced with the huge fee that Villa paid for his services and fans still felt sore after the poor displays against their arch rivals and newly promoted Newcastle United that season.

When Sunderland played Hibernian away in pre-season 2011, everyone, including the board and fans, could see that Asamoah Gyan was carrying the same characteristics and negative energy that Bent was showing before he handed in his transfer request. He looked overweight and uninterested in being part of Bruce's future plans. Gyan was eventually released by Bruce and joined an unheard of Middle East team called Al-Ain in a bizarre deal that became the most expensive loan signing in the world at the time. So now what Bruce was realistically looking at was both of his top signings Bent and Gyan lasting only a season and a half between them to move on to what they believed to be bigger and brighter career paths. The loss of these two players really affected the relationship between the manager and the owner.

Mark Douglas from *The Journal* said: "It seemed that there was a genuine affection between the pair. But Quinn's love for the game was sullied by the actions of Bent and Gyan, both of whom appeared to be motivated by money and ambition. Bruce had built a good side in the 2010–11 season but it was built on quicksand – and they had to start all over again the following season. In my opinion, the fault-lines were exposed when Short's knowledge of football and authority grew. He took over Sunderland as a greenhorn but began to question Bruce's purchases and results as the initial magic wore off. Quinn could protect Bruce, but only for so long."

Sunderland, yet again, completely revamped the team in the pre season of 2011–12 season with Bruce signing a total of 12 players. He went for a mixture of experience with John O'Shea and Wes Brown from his beloved Manchester United and youth with Connor Wickham, James McClean, and South Korean, Ji Dong-Won in his transfer activity.

The season started brightly with a fantastic equalising goal from Sebastian Larsson, another new addition, against Liverpool at Anfield on the opening day. However, the season took a massive turn for the worse for the club and was the second nail in Bruce's coffin, when the Sunderland manager's home-town team and Sunderland's arch rivals, came to the Stadium and beat his newly formed team 1–0 thanks to a Ryan Taylor free kick. Just when every-one was trying to forget the shocking efforts put in against the Magpies last season, they went and beat us again to send reverberations around the club.

The timing of the first north-east Derby of the season, offered Steve Bruce no favours at all, the hotly contested fixture coming in Sunderland's first home game of the season – an unusal occurence in the history of the rivalry. Had the disappointing loss been dished out half way through the season, perhaps after a decent run in the top flight, would this have softened the wounding blow somewhat? As it happened though, the huge loss in the first home game, meant Bruce was up against it for the rest of the season and the fans were not prepared to let him forget this result.

Steve Bruce, a man who always said that being from Tyneside would never interfere with his role, was now in the mire and a home defeat to bottom of the league and his former club Wigan was the final straw in the Sunderland manager's career. The fans were on his back and brought his roots up by singing offensive songs to show the under-fire boss that he was no longer required to lead the club in the right direction, the final whistle greeted with a chorus of boos and the end was nigh.

Niall Quinn was always friendly with the media, and maybe too friendly towards Steve Bruce, some arguing he could not bring up the courage to fire a man who he trusted so much as manager and as a friend. Graeme Bailey of *Sky Sports* agreed by saying: "Quinn as ever was diplomatic and thoroughly professional in his dealings and Bruce's removal was done without the club being dragged through the mire."

The end of the Bruce regime seemed to be a decision from the frustrated newly established owner, Ellis Short as Mark Douglas noticed: "By the start of the 2011–12 season, Quinn was on his way out. It was a personal decision but it looked from the outside as if he had been marginalised. We all knew it and though Sunderland denied it – very forcefully, in most instances – rumours that the chairman didn't have much longer did the rounds and it seemed clear that Short had taken a decision to get to grips with the finances of the club again.

It didn't seem to me as if he had been particularly impressed with the way Bruce had sought to overhaul the squad in successive summers and when the results at the start of the season didn't improve, Short grew impatient. After the Wigan game, where Bruce was subjected to fierce criticism from the stands, Short had made his decision but still, the briefing from Quinn was that the manager would get time.

A few papers ran a story saying Sunderland "would pause for breath" and not take a quick decision on Bruce's future. It smacked of a Quinn briefing but the next day Bruce was gone. Quinn had not been able to stop Short from pulling the trigger on his friend."

It was time for Bruce to go, whilst Quinn must have pondered what next for him at Sunderland.

Chapter Nine
The beginning of the end

Kelly Leigh Cooper, Stephen Linsley and Mal Robinson

After the sacking of Steve Bruce, new Chairman, Ellis Short took no time in replacing the Geordie manager and with the help of Niall Quinn, Sunderland finally got their man in Martin O'Neill. O'Neill was a manager the club had always been heavily linked with throughout the years, with the Northern Irishman's links to supporting Sunderland as a child, often mooted amongst the media, whenever the managerial hot seat at the Stadium of Light became vacant. The old midwife's tale of O'Neill even sporting a Sunderland tattoo, would also accompany such fresh media impetus on connecting O'Neill and Sunderland, which was of course, wide of the mark.

Quinn at this stage was 'Head of International Development', with many in the media and the Irish man himself citing the new 'Financial Fair Play' rulings, as justification for the switching of roles from Chairman to heading the club's 'International Development' scheme, although not primarily linked with his complete vanishing from Sunderland (despite the role not exactly being perpetual). Darlington, Luton Town, Glasgow Rangers and Portsmouth all being prominent examples of recent financial football catastrophes and an increasing number of clubs in the red throughout Europe, prompted UEFA to take action and introduce 'Financial Fair Play'. The books would be checked in the summer of 2012. Clubs would now have to spend within their means, moreover there would be a future break-even assessment covering the financial years ending 2012 and 2013 assessed during 2013–14, to assure that European clubs were abiding by the system, and if breached punishments would be imposed. Whether the alteration of Quinn's role was to bring in more revenue from abroad, or to give accomplished businessman Ellis Short the task of sorting the club's outgoings in preparation for Financial Fair Play, only those on the inside of the corridors of power at the Stadium of Light will know.

Yet with the arrival of O'Neill, the founder of the 'magic carpet ride' experience, thought it time to jump off with the emphasis on his job done, Niall leaving Sunderland in February 2012... for good.

Quinn's reasons for leaving the club are unlike his unconquerable personality, often questioned. No one is completely certain why he left, but nor is anyone oblivious and everyone tries to put their finger on why the departure came about. There are several avenues of reason for why the big man first left his position as Chairman of the football club, and then severing any official ties he had with Sunderland AFC, by vacating his role as Head of International Development.

The repositioning of Niall Quinn from the role of chairman into the accumulating new global business to the club was a contradictory one to all sentiments said of the man previously. For being a man admittedly more football-minded than business one it seemed strange for him to be re-designated into a role which required more boardroom prowess, than football nous.

What made Niall successful as chairman was his resonating passion for the club and area alike, he made a connection with the fans – the club had a family-like atmosphere. Quinn was seen as an 'insider', somebody who understood the passion of the locals and had seen previously the club at its pinnacle of late Nineties success from the forefront of being striker in a beamingly-full Stadium of Light. Niall swooped in on his imagined 'magic carpet' ride and swept us romanticised fans along with him. In him faith was almost unquestionable; Roy Keane, an inexperienced but unarguable leader, was put at the helm almost unchallenged and under him the dream began to be realised as once again Sunderland returned to the top flight. The ride was turbulent, had hitches, undoubtedly, but always Quinn seemed the nucleus; professed by Martin O'Neill at his departure as 'Mr Sunderland'.

Throughout the six years of Quinn's re-involvement with the club, this family atmosphere was not just felt amongst the fans; but within the staff too. There was a canon of integral members working behind the scenes who were affiliated with the Drumaville and Quinn movement in the re-imagining of the previously tired club. But pre-empting Quinn's 'side-stepping' role, long-term boardroom members were relieved of their positions, being replaced by Shorts' own preferences of Per Magnus Andersson and Mike Farnan, with Margaret Byrne gaining greater responsibility as CEO of the club. The boardroom changes were clinical and marked a consolidation of power by Short and a tightening of the reigns of the club he had ploughed so much of his funds into.

The intimate nature of club/fan relationship was being curtailed slowly. The 'Banqueting Suite' situated underneath the West Stand and helm of all things corporate of the club was no longer graced with Quinn during the Man of the Match presentations. Previously, for several years he had done a post-match speech to the room and helped in the presentation of gifts to sponsors and the post-match awards themselves. He was replaced by Kevin Ball and now by club legend and ambassador Jimmy Montgomery. Our new chairman is somewhat reclusive but the passionate connection still remains first through Martin O'Neill and now Paolo Di Canio at the helm.

Niall, an adopted mackem of sorts, always knew what was required to make connection with the fans. A deep affiliation and mutual understanding between him and the supporters was there from the outset. Sunderland is a passionate region full of passionate fans and the excuse-laden Steve Bruce was a far cry from what was wanted. The media and Bruce himself blamed fan prejudice against his 'Geordie' roots, but as a club whose most famed manager, in Bob Stokoe, was an ex 'Mag', the truth could not be further from the claims. Bruce, quiet natured and red faced had limited communication skills, seemingly not just in his relationship to the fans, but the players too. Although the pattern of prolific mercenary strikers escaping from our grasps can't be solely blamed on him, the man-management skills of the man have to be questioned, as far as a heading a club pushing for European football was concerned. We hit a terrible run of form two consecutive seasons under Bruce but still Quinn, the gentle giant, stuck with the man in whom he had instilled his trust, despite calls for more ruthless action from the vast majority of fans, disillusioned with extensive periods of dire results and performances.

There was a sort of stalemate alliance with Bruce that Quinn seemed at ease with, which was only relinquished when Quinn's chairman role was too. Short, apprenticed by Quinn, showed decisive action where Quinn wouldn't. Short, having heavily personally invested, like he did with Keane, demanded more commitment and success from his club and its manager. The sheer amount of players bought and sold within Keane and Bruce's tenures meant that stability was lacking, it was all very erratic. Some high-price purchases paid off, others didn't. We needed something more stable, long-term and tenable in order to progress as a club.

The appointment of O'Neill was seen as destined – for us fans at least. For years we've willed him to come and take helm at the club he 'supported' while young. Although Quinn wasn't the Chairman at the time of nego-tiations, he was said to have greatly influenced the appointment. Upon his agreement, O'Neill commented in regards to Quinn 'In many aspects, having talked with Niall, I think his role hasn't changed a great deal'. So why the shift to an 'international development role'?

From the outset, Quinn was said to have a five-year plan, to take us from the foot of the Championship to pushing towards the European spots, and in some senses by the end of his tenure this could be arguably achieved. The man is undoubtedly a local legend; for not once but twice selling our club with pure engrained passion and belief he has for us. In bringing in Short, he'd groomed him into the successor he wished to be taken over by, the legacy he wanted to leave behind. Perhaps it was by choice his role was slowly lessened then relieved like the official statements suggested. But there was undoubtedly a change in his stance the last couple of months. Weary and tired of the belligerent reluctance of some fans to commit long term, despite comparatively low season ticket prices, but a recessive econ-omy, investigations into the reasons behind a non-correlating attendance levels to increased league position were implemented. According to Quinn in a February 2011 statement, the conclusions of an independent investiga-tion was that 'the illegal showing of Saturday 3pm fixtures involving Sun-derland has an extremely detrimental effect on our attendances' and Quinn began a campaign to persuade these fans into spending there money not in local pubs, but in fact in the club itself, of which he had put so much in.

TV and live football: it is a pairing, arguably both hindering and aiding the evolution of modern football. Broadcasting means big bucks business and clubs profit massively from allowing the television cameras in. 'By-the-billion' oversees broadcasting rights for the Premier League, as well as domestic purchasing by companies such as Sky and ESPN equals a lot of generated income for the clubs involved. The Premier League, unlike other European ones such as La Liga, sells the rights to their games as a package rather than by individual fixtures, which helps prevent extreme polarization in the fees paid to top clubs as opposed to lesser 'appealing' ones. But with these televised sales comes a cost to the more traditional components of the 'beautiful game', perhaps to the games' actual attending gate. Of course for the larger clubs this risk is lessened by their huge global appeal and other 'glory-hunting' supporters both within and outside the catchment area meaning tickets will always be in demand. But for clubs such as ourselves, further away from the capital and without as much International appeal or exposure, the televising of our games has a history of diverting fans (and their ticket fees) away, instead opting for the cheaper options of watching in a pub or at home.

This was ex-Chairman and forever-Messiah Niall Quinn's problem when he launched a tirade not against officially licensed Sky broadcasters impact, but toward those fans who attended pubs with access to 'dodgy' foreign channels which have the ability to show almost every Premier League game instead of coming to cheer the lads on at home. He claimed (when being quoted as saying he 'despised' our fans who, despite having the financial capability to attend home games, instead opted to watch in a pub) that they were 'actually damaging the progress of the club' through diverting their spending elsewhere. Whether they were/are actually doing so can of course be argued over fiercely, it's unquestionable though that our average attendances have slumped somewhat since we were last in a comparative league positioning at the turn of the Millennium. But how much of that can really be blamed on television? Perhaps the record points total seasons really did turn many apathetic fans from avid followers into armchair observers? I know a few who still have not returned to buy another season ticket since. Still though, Sunderland's average home attendance in the 2007–08 season, after that, in Keane's debut Premier League managing season, was still a few thousand more that a couple of years ago under Bruce. So neither hypothesis gives conclusive proof of what is keeping fans away. The big four, or rather now five or six, have a disproportionate amount of games televised in the UK and you just have to look around locally to see their 'fans' swearing their 'allegiance' to them up here: children in Chelsea strips emblazoned with 'Drogba' wandering around Sunderland; they aren't Stamford Bridge regulars, does this mean they're harming 'their' club? Is it really so bad to watch on TV rather than attend? Fans of mid table clubs like Sunderland going to pubs to watch our games on foreign channels, are arguably just attaining the same access as 'big four' 'supporters' have to be able to watch games regularly in pubs or on the computer at home.

Away from the attendance and foreign broadcast debates, the actual filming and broadcasting of football has undoubtedly altered the game massively since *BskyB* bought the Premier League rights in 1992. Football is big business now probably mainly because of Sky Sports' influence, the game is subject to hyperinflation as advertising investors pour billions into it, realising the big-money potential and the global exposure the Premier League can bring. It is not harmonious though; officials and players now come under more scrutiny that ever, with replays being readily available to undermine both constantly. The game is now pacier and more skillful than ever, with slow motion replays often focusing on 'show-boating' individual skill, individually making cult celebrity status of the Individual, rather than working for the overall success of a team. Think of the Ballotelli hype; would the myth and appeal surrounding him be so great without televised football?

Quinn had always been vocal; a popular media figure he wasn't shy of Sky and their interviewing cameras. We were used to him being outspoken and making the collective voice of Sunderland heard, or giving us titbits for transfer knowledge. But the statement released by him that he 'despised' a substrate of our fans was reckless and took a lot of fans aback. Perhaps it was a display of his frustration that the measures to increase attendances was failing? It was worded strongly to attract media attention, which it achieved. PR wise, it wasn't very professional and it was hardly likely to entice those straying fans back. He said he felt no anger towards those who genuinely couldn't afford to attend; however persistently the club and Quinn seemed to largely ignore external factors such as the state of the economy itself and similar issues with attendance were occurring nation-ally. Ultimately dropped attendances cannot be attributed to a few local clubs using foreign satellite channels alone. The reaction wasn't the one he anticipated, and it clearly in retrospect seems like a mistake, an own goal of sorts. The damage it did is debatable; but the man's achievement and commitment to both the club and local area was not likely to be undone with one silly press release. His heart has always been with us, and nothing vindictive was meant in his statements, all he's ever wanted is glory for the club he became enchanted with, it just came at an unfortunate timing with poor form and disenchantment with the Steve Bruce tenure.

However, never before had the great man been questioned by his own supporters, or those who did were deemed to be fools. But with a full house served up with a dire display in a 2–0 defeat at home to Liverpool in March, and an abomination of a home record throughout the calendar year of 2011, it was becoming an increasingly arduous task to agree with Quinn on his arguably incongruous comments. In fact following the article of him blasting the 'Pub Fans', Sunderland had won just two games until his resignation as Chairman in October 2011. The deficiency of value for money Sunderland's home support was receiving, was beginning to justify fans dispatching their pay packets elsewhere than the Stadium of Light. Perhaps watching the match inebriated in a pub was a far more appealing option than watching absolute dross in matches against the likes of; Liver-pool, Fulham and Wolves with no intoxicant, if you couldn't afford both alcohol and match ticket, which seemed to be the excuse of many.

Season ticket revenue or ticket sales, although being important to clubs, aren't the main major financial contributor to their revenue. Our revenue in 2011, of £64 million, was nowhere near some of the other Premier League levels. Because of our geographical location, in Northern England and lack of real success over the last four decades, Sunderland aren't attractive on an international scale like other Premier League clubs are. Perhaps upon real-ising this; and with the possibly stale boardroom being revived with people with great business acumen, this implemented the changes we've seen in the club, attempting to appeal more to foreign markets over the last year or two, such as South Korea, Africa and Hong Kong.

A reason too, it seemed in the creation of the 'international development' role for Niall in October 2011, the deal with 'Invest in Africa' as shirt sponsors for Sunderland described as 'ground-breaking' by then Vice-chairman and Labour MP, David Milliband, could be argued as fruits of our attempt at expansion abroad. 'Tullow Oil' was the founding partner of the initiative, as Africa's dominant independent oil company, and although the main purpose for the campaign is promoting investment in the continent; it does a lot to introduce Sunderland to the territory. O'Neill in an interview said it would put us more so on the 'international stage' and Texan chairman Short said that 'we all want for the club to continue to prosper and to expand its global audience.' The deal has not been without criticism though; concerns were raised at the practices of the founding company, who denied full disclosure of the details of all their contracts and deals. There are claims that Tullow Oil damaged local business, with their soaring profit increases of 600% since launching the 'invest in Africa Campaign'. The shirt sponsorship deals' worth was estimated at an enormous £20million, equaling those of both Manchester clubs and Liverpool and trumping Chelsea's deal with Samsung. It was a major coup for the club, Niall at the launch of the initiative said that, "If there was a Champions' League for commitment to community development, Sunderland Football Club would be the European champions".

When Quinn came into the newly coined position, chairman Short claimed that 'it is essential for the long-term success of the club we develop interests on a global scale'. Yet after just four months in the job, when Quinn resigned from the club as a whole; the position was absolved and no replacement was sought. The couple of months Quinn spent in this ambiguously purposed role seem to be that of an 'easing out' period. Quinn was so pivotal with the changing of the club from a national joke, with near consecutive lowest point total relegations, to a relatively consolidated Premier League force. With Quinn, and the ownership movement of the club, things felt somewhat grassroots. Fans felt involved; Quinn is interpreted as a fan, of sorts, himself. The people owning the club, although undoubtedly all being rich entrepreneurs and successful in their respective industries, felt identifiable. It wasn't an anonymous foreign investor looking to use the club as a plaything for bored excess. The original Drumaville consortium was made up of almost pals of our big Irishman. Charlie Chawke one of the investors, was often seen drinking in the Sports Bar inside of the stadium alongside fans. It all felt friendly and accessible. Even after the eventual buying out of Drumaville entirely by Short; faith remained because it was Niall who had procured his investment.

At the time Quinn's role was altered and Short replaced him, there was much emphasis in club statements playing down the changes, Short assured the fans that 'it's the same group of people continuing to lead the club.' In reality though, it wasn't. From boardroom to hospitality level, major reshaping was going on behind the scenes as the façade of normality was retained through the maintenance of the figurehead of Quinn as an integral part of the club. It was only when the talisman fan desired manager of O'Neill was secured that it was safe for Quinn's eventual departure to be revealed. He had been sidelined undoubtedly, and gently eased out of a role that in reality he didn't have the business credentials to maintain. Not in a negative way, the man is known within the football community for his warm and open nature, his brutal honesty and within the area, his passion and love for the club. This, although leaving us enviable from people who feel disenfranchised for the running of the club, left his role untenable. Football nowadays isn't what it was, and you have to be clinical to be successful. Like it or lump it, the financial element is integral to the game.

Quinn wasn't driven by profit, for years and years he maintained his ambition to see a full stadium rather than huge revenues. We have some of the most competitive pricing structures in the country and frequently have on offers and deals to help tempt punters in, because of the economic circumstance of the catchment area of the city of Sunderland and the Wearside area in general. According to the Sunderland City centre website, a quarter of the city's children live in relative poverty. Unemployment in Sunderland currently sits around 6%, way above the national average. The north-east of England, especially Sunderland, lags behind in its employment and education opportunities. The Foundation of Light, the club's registered charity obviously does a lot to work with the local area, and Quinn as head of it for a long period of time, was heavily involved with schemes such as 'Niall's Mile', which helped raise money for the cause which invests into the local area.

Despite its inarguable red and white elements, the man has a heart of gold. He was the first player to donate the proceeds of his 2002 testimonial game to charity; and changed the nature of the affairs forever. The £1 million made was shared between the Sunderland hospital children's ward and other causes in Ireland, Asia and Africa. He's directly and indirectly raised millions for charity and his contribution to the local community is staggering.

The Sunderland Stadium of Light now is also classed as a major music venue as well as footballing cathedral, thanks in part to Niall's vision of having regular music concerts in the close season of every campaign, allowing the north-east region to enjoy a bonanza pay day each summer as a result. With such global musical names as Oasis, Coldplay, Bruce Springsteen, Take That and Bon Jovi, all holding gigs on Wearside, the local vicinity continues to reap the financial rewards of Quinn's forward thinking in utilising Sunderland's 49,000 seater stadium all year round and will continue to do so, years after Niall has left the club.

If you'd have said Quinn's tenure on the Sunderland board had been anything less than successful, no doubt any fan, board member, or indeed anyone with a hint of knowledge on Sunderland's recent history alike would correct you by pointing out where we were even in the days before his arrival as chairman, and rightly so. 'A magic carpet ride' it may not have appeared to Sunderland fans with immeasurable expectations, but stabilising the football club at the top level of English football for its longest spell since the mid 1960s, was seen by the vast majority of our support as a miracle. A monumental stepping-stone across the river to where Sunderland AFC could once again prove themselves amongst the elite. You would just have to comprehend where the club was and where it was heading at the climax of the 2005–06 season, to contemplate what Niall Quinn did for us off the pitch.

Niall himself, and his turn around in his fortunes as a player, is almost an allegory for the tale of our beloved club itself. He came in under Peter Reid, he was lanky and out much of his first season due to injury. He was the club record signing and everyone thought he was ultimately, a bit useless, a letdown. But against all odds, he, the haggard underdog, blighted with two serious injuries, came back and was the latter half of a famously successful 'little and large' strike force which would become one of the most famed in the history of Sunderland AFC. He galvanised our players after the play off final defeat, sharing his experience with the younger pups. He was never the most famous in the Premier League or well known as a player, but he stuck in through rough times with grit and lead the way.

Quinn and Phillips together, were adored by the inhabitants of the newly built Stadium of Light. In their heyday they provided the 'good times' of recent Sunderland history. It would never be forgotten by Quinn. When Sunderland needed him, when they needed someone to give them a chance, against all odds, he did it. He pulled it off. He galvanised and dragged together a mixed bag of Irishman who were mad enough to plough in millions to a club on its back legs, crippled by debt, embarrassed by relegation with the record lowest points total. He flew in, not on a magic carpet, but in a light aircraft into Newcastle Airport, live on *Sky Sports News*. Those long, gangly legs in a pair of suspiciously high-waisted white trousers, getting out of the doorway and uttering those words, 'I'm here to see Bob tonight. I'm hoping to close up a deal with him' to, with his consortium, buy Sunderland AFC. The comparison about Drumaville having a 'good hand' at poker reflects the gamble he was taking in buying such a sorry stated club.

The smile on his face when he sat there in a press conference unveiling, of all people, Roy Keane as his manager (after the blip of Niall attempting the job himself). He worked his backside off for Sunderland; when he didn't owe us anything. He gave us goals, he gave us leadership as a club captain, he gave our region's sick children money that he didn't have to. Yet still, he came back. The man won't be remembered here for the bad times during the period: like the 5–1 derby defeat, his attempt at a managerial sinking us like a dead weight to the foot of the Championship or careless comments to the press. He will be remembered as the saviour of this football club; the man who dared to believe in us when nobody else would. Who convinced dozens of others to do so and with their own money. He tried to show them why he fell in love with Sunderland, the club whose endless trudging lows are eclipsed entirely by the little but ultimate highs. The little sparks of against all odds victories. He wasn't in it for the money. He cared and still does care about Sunderland AFC. We are his Sunderland. We are the club we are now because of him. He gave his time beyond the necessary; he sat in working men's clubs around the local area, face to face with the working class fans, explaining his ambitions and the need for commitment in the form of season ticket sales. His exit was subdued, a far cry from the excitement felt in the early days, he ghosted his way out of the back door just as the party got in full swing; tireless work paying off in the form of consolidating us as a Premier League club within the safe grasps of Martin O'Neill and Ellis Short, amongst others.

With his departure, we've lost what we had. The feeling of closeness and passion and being able to turn on the sports news and see him saying probably a little bit too much in interviews, and giving a little too much away. But he left Sunderland in hands he believes capable. We're okay now. We're not world-beaters. It's not going to be three points every week. It is Sunderland after all. It's going to come, like it always has, probably with more lows than highs. Yet just remember, in the end, that those highs make it all worth it, as the man Quinn himself pointed out when he left the club that darkest of Februarys in 2012.

"I've had the most amazing six years. It gives me a huge sense of pride to see where the club is today. Everything is in place for Sunderland to really make a statement, which was always my aim."

It had been the ultimate football romance between Niall Quinn and Sunderland AFC, which began back in 1996, when the Irish international striker became Peter Reid's marquee signing of the summer. Fast forward 17 years and Quinn's name is as set in stone in Sunderland history, as the concrete foundations holding up the Stadium of Light.

Perhaps one day there maybe a new statue outside the ground, next to the current Bob Stokoe monument, celebrating the manager messiah, who won the FA Cup against all odds for Sunderland back in 1973. The new statue may not mirror the image of a manager running across the Wembley turf to congratulate his goalkeeper, as Stokoe did in '73, but it will have the following testimonial etched into it, just under the stone based magic carpet.

"Niall Quinn, honourary MBE, footballer who appeared for Sunderland 220 times with 69 goals, first goalscorer at the Sunderland Stadium of Light, first player to score a hat-trick at the Stadium of Light, Championship winner in 1999, goalscorer of the winning goal in a north-east Derby, striker and occasional goalkeeper, who then took control of Sunderland as Chairman in 2006, became temporary Manager and helped ultimately save the club, setting Sunderland on a steady course of top flight football not seen since the 1960s."

Chapter Ten
Niall Quinn – The Opinion
and The Legacy

In this unique publication of a collection of tributes and analysis of the Niall Quinn story at Sunderland, what better way to conclude than gain the reflection of former players and team mates, fans, writers, press and business leaders alike, all in unison in their support of the man known as Mr Sunderland.

"I would say he was the most genuine person I have ever met in football and probably in life! He was and still is a real honest guy, very down to earth, but get him on a football pitch and over that white line and he was a different person, with a will to win for his team.

His influence rubbed off on many people, whilst I had the fortune to play with Niall. It is safe to say all Premier League sides, make that any football team would love a side comprising of eleven Niall Quinns.

It's a shame to see him not involved anymore at Sunderland and what is their loss will be someone else's gain, I am sure."

Michael Gray, former team mate.
Sunderland AFC 1992–2004.

"On my first day Niall Quinn walked up to this young kid, shook my hand, put his arm around my shoulder and welcomed me to Sunderland AFC. He always made himself available to me. My cruciate injury hit me hard and I spent a long time injured, the injury kept me away from home and off the pitch for nine months and to a young lad that is hard.

The gaffer (Peter Reid) was good to me and let me go back to Blackpool for a while but it was Quinny that really helped me out. He had

had both knees repaired so knew what I was going through, he made sure he was on hand to help and encourage me with my physio.

Working with Quinny was great, he was always encouraging and talking to the younger players. 'Get it up the pitch to me', 'take your time', 'enjoy yourself' always positive and getting the very best from those around him. I am sure everyone on Wearside loves this man, he was great as a player and tremendous as the chairman. There is no doubting the love the area has for him and he has for the club and the fans.

I was privileged to pull on the garters on my socks at his testimonial and it was a very proud moment for him and an honour to share the night with him and his family."

Gavin McCann, former team mate.
Sunderland AFC, 1998–2003.

"His time at the club was like a whirlwind romance that seemed to last for a long time but ended abruptly before you had the chance to step back and appreciate what he did for the club. It's not just his achievements that should be applauded but his charity work in the region and promoting the city and the club to the international market.

He will be remembered as a committed player and for his famous little and large partnership with Kevin Phillips, this wasn't enough for him though. Coming back to become chairman and run the club during one of their lowest points in our history was always going to be a risk to his cult status achieved as a player but he made bold statements from the beginning which he delivered upon.

Another added bonus is the Stadium of Light has become an established music concert venue. With the likes of Oasis, Bruce Springsteen and Red Hot Chili Peppers in town in recent years, this has brought income from tourism and puts the City of Sunderland on the map. He has helped make Sunderland football club attractive not just to established well known football players but to the music industry, businesses and other club's football fans.

I can't help thinking whether Steve Bruce should have been sacked earlier than he did as the players lost direction, a bad winless run had occurred and the gap between the manager and the fans was getting bigger all the time. During his tenure, towards the end the atmosphere amongst Sunderland fans was very low, confidence in the manager had gone. Although loyalty was one of Niall's qualities and he always backed his managers in public, you can argue he could have been more ruthless with Bruce but then there was more stability at the club than at many others which is a good thing.

Niall Quinn understands not just the club but the fans and the region, an ambassadorial role would have been fitting for the big man. His influence, charisma and knowledge of the club will be missed. He was able to engage with all kinds of people, that's his biggest strength. He was also honest and thought he could do no more and perhaps felt it was someone else's turn to lead the club, making sure the right person came along first.

I did not personally meet the big man, but a good friend has. She approached Quinny outside the stadium and Niall asked how she was and if she was looking forward to the game. She even had a photograph taken with him. Every time we talk about Niall Quinn she brings up her encounter with him outside the Stadium of Light. Always made time to chat to the fans.

His time at the club was mesmerising for the fans and region, it's not like he became chairman and ran the club like any old business. This was not just a job, it was a passion and his duty to serve the club he loves."

Nathan Johnson, Editor in Chief,
Sunderland World

"Niall Quinn for me is the most important person in the history of SAFC since its founder James Allan. On the playing side he put his ageing injury ravaged body on the line for Sunderland time after time.

The big Dubliner scored many memorable goals in a never to be forgotten partnership with fellow striker Kevin Phillips. The three games of many that stand out for me were the two 2–1 victories at the Wonga Dome (St James' Park) where Niall scored on each occasion and the two superb goals during an outstanding display in a 4–1 win against Chelsea at the Stadium of Light. Quinny also proved his versatility when he went in goal at Bradford City and kept a clean sheet in a 1–0 victory for Sunderland in a vital promotion game.

Then he brought a group of seven Irish businessman together including Charlie Chawke and Louis Fitzgerald along with Hays Travel owner John Hays to form Drumaville named after a tiny village in Co. Donegal, Ireland the magic carpet was launched.

Niall said he wanted to re–connect with the fans and this he certainly did, especially the fantastic gesture when he paid for taxi's for Sunderland supporters stranded at Bristol Airport on a Saturday night on their way back from seeing SAFC play at Cardiff City. That will rarely be seen again in modern football.

I live fairly close to the "Niall Quinn Children Centre" in Kayll Road, Sunderland and this legacy sums up the big man for me.

The selfless act of giving the proceeds of his benefit match to worthy causes tells you all you need to know of the type of man Niall Quinn is. I remember the day of his benefit match talking to fans over from Ireland together with Manchester City and Celtic fans who had travelled to be part of such a great occasion. The idea to have non-match tickets for £10 so people who could not make the match was also an inspired idea.

Quinny's commitment to the SAFC Foundation of Light (Sunderland AFC's official charity) also deserves a mention. Niall was always a big supporter of the Foundation and I believe he still makes donations towards it and Niall's Mile, which involves Sunderland schoolchildren and people of all ages walking to raise money for the Foundation is another legacy that Niall has left our City.

Some might say that the appointment of Steve Bruce was a poor decision but I think at the time given Bruce's track record particularly at Wigan, it appeared to be a good move. However maybe Bruce could have been sacked earlier.

There was a lot controversary over Niall Quinn having a go at so called 'fans' who watch home matches in pubs in Sunderland and surrounding areas, instead of attending the Stadium of Light. I actually think Quinn was spot on with his comments and did not deserve the criticism he received over this.

I certainly think Niall Quinn should have been given at least an ambassador's role. When you think of his track record of helping to attract the likes of Roy Keane, Martin O'Neill, Boylesports, Drumaville, Ellis Short and Invest in Africa proves the guy oozes charisma and always speaks highly of the club.

While I feel that the Quinn's Bar named in honour of Niall is a nice touch I feel that something further should be done to recognise all that the great man has done for our club. Perhaps a stand named after him or a statue at the ground would be a nice touch, but Quinny wouldn't want the attention!

Three (of many) stories spring to mind when I think of Niall. One was when I was in hospitality at the stadium during Niall's playing days at the club. It was back in the day when the *Sunderland Echo* used to invite fans to vote for their "Player of the Month" and if the panel agreed with your selection and your name came came out of the hat then you won and would be guest of the club for a match. This happened to me when I voted for Quinny and I was lucky enough to win the prize. The match was against Leeds United and Niall was out injured at the time and was working for Sky Sport as it was their live match.

About twenty minutes before the kick off Niall introduced himself to me and apologised for not spending more time with me but as he had been working for Sky he was unable to. He then asked me what my plans were after the match and arranged to meet me in "Durty Nellys" which was part of the Mowbray Park Hotel in those days. I was also in the company of my brother and Niall proceeded to buy all our drinks for the rest of the night and he could not have been any friendlier or charming.

On another occasion I was in Ashbrooke Sports Club one Sunday afternoon and I had heard that there was going to be a charity Gaelic football match involving Irish students at Sunderland University and Irish players from SAFC's Academy.

Much to my great surprise as it turned out there were SAFC first team players Kevin Kilbane, Jason McAteer and Niall Quinn there along with the younger players such as Tommy Butler, Brendan McGill, Stephen Capper, Cliffy Byrne and Mark Rossister – all Irish youngsters at the time. I watched from the window and saw Niall and company playing in freezing monsoon conditions. Post match Quinny was his usual charming self; having his photo taken and signing an abundance of autographs as by the end of the match word had spread about what was happening in the middle-class leafy Ashbrooke and quite a crowd had gathered. By all accounts SAFC Manager Peter Reid was furious with Niall as one of the senior pros involved as he had not had the match approved with Reidy!

The third story again involved drink! I was in the Burton House pub in the East End area of Sunderland one Sunday and in walked about a dozen or so guys including Niall Quinn and former players – Richard Ord, Micky Gray and local boxer Billy Hardy. While some of the group were looking a bit worse for wear drink wise you wouldn't have thought Quinny had touched a drop. The Live match was Aberdeen v Celtic and Niall asked me to keep him updated with the score while Micky Gray and Billy Hardy were having an arm wrestling contest on the pool table and Quinny was the referee! Of course a couple of drinks arrived at the bar courtesy of Mr Disco Pants which I hadn't even asked for.

Martin O'Neill rightly described Quinny as Mr Sunderland and he will always have huge respect amongst Sunderland supporters. Every Sunderland fan that you will have met loves Niall. Personally as a Sunderland fan of many years I will always be grateful for what he has done for Sunderland and for our City. He is a living Legend who can always hold his head up high in Sunderland."

Tony Ratton,
Lifetime Sunderland fan.

"It is a puzzle often posed yet seldom solved – just what constitutes legend in football? Take Niall Quinn, for example. He was a good striker, but he wasn't anything special. He was an atrocious manager, albeit a caretaker one. As a chairman, in tangible terms he didn't actually achieve much more than his predecessor. In cold terms and just about every measurable way, his achievements at Sunderland were nothing remarkable, yet he is – absolutely and irrevocably – a legend.

All the ingredients are there, I suppose. The reluctant protagonist, who overcomes early adversity to swoop in and save the day just when all looked lost, then vanishes off into the sunset with a quiet dignity. A classic hero for a classic tale.

I can still vividly remember the beginning of that tale, which I always found somewhat strange given its inauspicious nature. I recall the photograph of Quinn towering over Peter Reid whilst shaking his hand on the Roker Park pitch that I noticed on the back of an English paper whilst on holiday in Spain. We had signed a donkey – that's what everyone said. I agreed with them.

An early lengthy injury-absence as the club suffered relegation did little to prompt a rethink. By the time he had put in an absolutely appalling performance at home to Norwich the following season in which he showed little evidence that he could even run never mind play football, I was certain the sorry affair would be over soon and our club would be rid of this expensive mistake. I have never been more wrong, and nor have I ever been happier to be wrong.

I suppose, however, that a large – almost seminal – part of what sets Quinn apart in the affections of us Sunderland fans is not so much what he did when he was here, but what he did when he wasn't.

The summer of 2006 was ugly. I have followed the lads through the Third Division and through the early 90s and beyond, but nothing quite compared to that summer. I speak to younger fans now quite regularly, and they moan about this and that and the other... our top class stadium is poorly stewarded, our £10m England International isn't quite firing yet, and our other winger committed a Twitter faux pas and the like.

There is a part of me that dearly wants to play the veteran card with them. Tell them that they don't know they are born and they should have been standing with me on the uncovered Roker Park terraces on a freezing winter night watching the likes of Martin Gray and Ian Sampson lump aimless long balls in the general direction of some no-hoper reserve forward we had begged Crystal Palace or someone similarly bland to loan us. *Then* they'd have had a football club to really moan about.

But the truth is that I know that if they saw that summer six and a half years ago then I have no right to lecture them about following Sunderland through grim times. If they saw that summer then they have looked upon as dark a sky as I have ever seen and if they still had the stomach to love the lads enough to moan about them today then they had absolutely nothing to prove to anyone. Well, their sanity to a properly trained mental health professional, perhaps, but certainly not me.

After all, there were plenty of fans who walked away entirely at that point and many more who never dared care for the club in quite the same way again. I suspect we all know someone to serve as an example of at least one of those. And yet, when people born into it were fleeing, Niall Quinn was desperate to abandon his cushy lifestyle and buy his way into the very heart of it because he thought he could make a difference.

He did make a difference too. It wasn't always plain sailing. In fact, at times it was downright miserable. I felt like throttling him myself the day he decided to gamble our extraordinarily hard-earned Premier League status on the managerial talents of Ricky Sbragia, but as tempting as it may be it is important that we don't fall into the trap of giving history a favourable rewrite because to do so would be to suggest that the truth is somehow not good enough. The Niall Quinn Sunderland story does not need to be embellished or given a glossy coat to be worth celebrating.

The big scraps he got right, however. It may not have always been graceful but, in true hero style, he got the job done. Roy Keane, for example, was the right man at the right time. His subsequent struggles at Ipswich showed that there was nothing inherently special about him as a manager. But the situation at Sunderland was simply uniquely tailored to him and Quinn knew that because he knew the club – his club.

In the end, you end up wondering if how well Quinn knew the club was ultimately what saw him leave it. From the moment he conceived of returning to the club, Martin O'Neill was the man he wanted at its helm. He recognized him as a man who shared his affinity with the support. It almost seems that being in a position to attract the former Celtic boss to Sunderland was a private barometer for knowing his work was done.

He himself may have seen that as his great final gift to the Sunderland support, but it is his legacy that will endure long after O'Neill's desk has been cleared. I've never been one for alternative history, so grandiose statements like 'Niall Quinn saved the club from oblivion' have always sat uncomfortably with me. I just don't know what would have happened to the club without Niall Quinn.

I know what *did* happen with him, though, and it's all I will ever need to know. He saw a club that had been beaten to such a bloody pulp and left in a heap on the floor that even those of us who loved it the most had difficulty identifying and, when others were ready to accept it, he took responsibility for healing the wounds and hauling it back onto its feet.

So what makes Niall Quinn a legend on Wearside? Quite simply, in an age when football is blighted with mercenaries, happy to sell their empty badge kissing to the highest bidder, Quinn is the man who genuinely cared. He chose Sunderland. There is no finer legacy – or more worthy legend – than that."

Michael Graham, Lifetime Sunderland fan.

In my own personal experiences involving the legend that is Niall Quinn, I found that he had a noticeable presence yet a humbling one; a presence that is rarely witnessed. In his early days as Chairman (and also as manager), I encountered the sky scraping Irishman as an admiring eleven-year-old at Newcastle Airport. The squad were in the early stages of the 2006–07 season and were travelling down to Southend United as the Coca Cola Championship's bottom side (a game which ended in a 3–1 loss at Roots Hall). Niall Quinn was very generous and an uplifting smile accompanied his directions to where the (rather less inspiring) Sunderland team were situated to litter my conveniently worn replica shirt with signatures. This is just one example of the man's warmness as a person, which he has shown throughout his time as player and chairman, from beginning to end. It was his personality that most probably charmed original and further investors to rid the club of its yo-yo label by investing heavily and Niall will be even more fondly regarded by Sunderland supporters because of this."

Stephen Linsley, *Seventy3* Writer and Sunderland fan.

"Not only was Niall a great player, probably the best ever in a lifetime of "Tall" players, but also a complete gentleman, who always had the time to speak with the fans and sign autographs, unlike many of todays players. *(Who incidentally need a reality check)*

I am amazed that the club have not renamed one of the stands after him, how many other people have done the following for our club: Exceptional player, Club Chairman, brought millions into the club through his connections, was instrumental in bringing Martin O'Neill, introduced the Drumaville Consortium "When we were in a sorry state" and sold the club to Ellis Short with his financial backing. Niall is a man who gave his heart and soul to our club, and also to local charities, and his name will never be forgotten on Wearside. With our stands having no particular naming in their current guise as the North, South, East and West Stands, surely it's time to rename one of then after Niall?

I don't think Niall made any mistakes, every decision he made was for the well being of the club, and we may still be in a sorry state, were it not for his tireless work, both on and off the pitch. If we were ever to get any other players of his stature, skill, and dedication SAFC would be an even greater club."
Gary SAFC Lamb,
Lifetime Sunderland fan.

"Niall Quinn was an exceptional ambassador for Sunderland Football Club, a chairman who drove the club out of difficult times and transformed its profile. Through his hard work and dedication, Sunderland is no longer perceived as the yo-yo club it once was.

He would have preferred to have led Sunderland to greater success on the pitch before deciding to leave, but the work he did do – on and off the pitch – will never be forgotten by anyone on Wearside.

He changed the profile of the club, took it to new levels internationally. Without Niall, the Drumaville consortium would never have got together to take over the club and Ellis Short is unlikely to have ever got himself involved. The true legacy of Quinn's time with the club is unlikely to be known until the effects of the Short era unfold. It could be that Sunderland are set for the greatest period in the club's history. If that proves to be the case then Quinn's influence and dedication during his time as chairman should never, and will never, be under-estimated.

There were mistakes made and he will be the first to admit that. However, it was the first time he had been a chairman of a football club. Perhaps the handling of the Roy Keane situation, with the manager's deteriorating relationship with Ellis Short, could have been handled better. Undoubtedly Keane's successor, Steve Bruce, was allowed to make too many changes to his squad year on year. The Darren Bent situation could also have been handled differently, with the striker effectively forcing through a move having spent months portraying the image of a striker in love with living in the area.

With time Quinn's position was always going to come to an end. Given how he had outlined a five-year plan at the beginning of his chairmanship, he actually got through that period of time. Once he had convinced Ellis Short to take over the club from the Dumaville Consortium, the goal posts had been moved. Despite turning to Quinn for advice, Short was always going to be the man making the big decisions, so with time a parting was always going to be necessary.

Whether Quinn was given an ambassadorial role or not, Sunderland fans will always appreciate what he did for the club. The Irishman and Sunderland will always have a lifelong association together, even if he doesn't have the title to prove it.

I will never forget the day I heard at *The Northern Echo* that Niall Quinn was flying in to the North East to have talks with outgoing Sunderland chairman Bob Murray. On putting the phone down, I drove straight to Durham Tees-Valley airport to see him arrive. I met him on the tarmac after the plane landed on the runway and rather than dismiss the intrusive reporter he was happy to inform and confirm readers of the talks.

Weeks later, after further detailed discussions, the deal was in place... that evening at the airport was where it was all began.

Whether he was a player, a manager or a chairman, Niall Quinn was always an absolute pleasure to deal with. It was a privilege to have the opportunities I had to interview and chat with him and he is genuinely one of the nicest people I have had the chance to interview in football.

Whatever happens from now on at Sunderland, Quinn did his best. His best may not have ended in a major piece of silverware, but undoubtedly he has helped take the club to a new level after years of instability in the latter stages of the Murray reign."
Paul Fraser, Chief Football Writer,
The Northern Echo.

"Niall Quinn was some player, I think he is, what, six foot seven tall? For someone so big he was very skilful, perhaps not the sharpest striker but with the ball on the floor he took some effort to get near. Being a centre-half I have played against some big lads, but Niall was very difficult to play against in training. He could hold it up, was great in the air and his touch was great.

It was easy to play with him, the 'keeper would kick it out and he would catch it on his toe and bring it down effortlessly. I loved watching him and Kevin Phillips play together, they were a great partnership.

As a man, he was a gentle giant, very friendly to everyone and always ready to tell a joke. His clothes were memorable, but for all the wrong reasons. On a night out he was always making sure everyone had fun, starting games to involve all the boys. He loved a game of cards or the horses and I found him to be a great friend to have around at all times.

He was great a leader on and off the pitch, I never saw him being a chairman but the position came along and he became a natural, if it was me buying the club I would have at least made sure I was manager for a few days too!

He left the famous song from his playing days strong on the fans memories, that is a humourous legacy and we sang it a few times.. 'Niall Quinn's disco pants...' but the fans have experienced Niall Quinn the fantastic player, chairman and I believe truly appreciate what this man has done for Sunderland the Football Club and the surrounding Wearside areas."

Jody Craddock, former team mate,
Sunderland AFC 1997–2003.

"I remember my very first game for Sunderland. It was Queen's Park Rangers at home and this was a big step up for me, in terms of attendance as I was used to a few thousand but now there was forty-five thousand fans in the Stadium of Light.

In Scandinavia the preparation is thoughtful, quiet and you go within yourself and you would not be seen joking or exchanging banter as such as in the UK. And so I was sat in the corner, nervous at my first game and also considering what may happen gazing down at my feet. Up comes Niall asking 'What's wrong? Are you OK?' and he told me to relax, liven up and enjoy the occasion. He was breaking the ice and supporting me, it really helped me to relax and took away all my nerves.

Niall was a leader on and off the pitch, he was always very clever and knew what he wanted to achieve for himself and his family.

We went on a team day, paint balling and in the morning we met at his house, it had some land for his horses and a lovely view. We sat eating bacon rolls and he just always seemed content. He never seemed materialistic and some say it showed in his clothes, but he always made you feel comfortable and very much at home around him.

He is one of the all-time legends of Sunderland AFC, no-one will forget his testimonial and how he gave it all to charity. He is a 'man of the fans', always respected request to sign this and take a picture. The fans were part of the team for him and as we all know he is a great team player.

Whenever I have the fortune to come back to the Stadium of Light he would come to the dressing room and say hello and ask if I needed anything, it is always a pleasure to run into him."
Thomas Sorensen, former team mate,
Sunderland AFC 1998–2003.

"There are many facets to Niall Quinn that are worth my writing about. The fact that he scored the first ever goal at the Stadium of Light against his former club, Manchester City is one option, or that he chose proper football over the silly "Aussie Rules" style is another.

I could even wax lyrical about his business acumen, which helped to save the club from financial doom.

All of these would make for great reading I'm sure, however, the Niall Quinn I chose to talk about is not the horse racing manager some know him as, nor the award-winning novelist others take him for.

No, I will be talking about Niall Quinn the "Emergency Goalkeeper".

It was in the distant past of 1999 that this event occurred. We were playing the illustrious Bradford City and Quinny had just scored what turned out to be the winning goal. Fantastic stuff. Yet, the scoreline was staring nervously down at us Black Cats – one-nil – when one of football's worst case scenarios occurred: our stalwart between the sticks, Thomas Sorensen, was stretchered off with all of thirteen minutes left to play.

With no one to replace him, the bad luck behind the number seemed all too real, until to the fans' disbelief, up stepped the Irish giant, goal-scoring, Disco-Panted, Niall Quinn to don the gloves.

The fans from Bradford were loving it – surely it would be a City goal-fest? Their centre-forward in the nets? No chance. Yet, it seemed the bad luck behind those thirteen minutes was not meant for us but for them, as little did they know, this wasn't the first time Mr Quinn played the role of goalkeeper.

For that we need to go even further back, to the pre-Etihad days of 1991, when the great man was wearing the light blue of Manchester City. His opponents this time were Derby County and the scenario almost identical: having scored early on, Quinn was playing a great game when Citeh's 'keeper, Tony Coton, was sent-off just before half-time, giving Derby a much-needed penalty.

As their tallest player, Quinn the obvious choice to replace Coton. Dean Saunders, the Ram's main goalscorer, stepped up to the spot only for Quinn to pull off a magnificent save. It was a huge moment in the match, securing a win for the boys in blue and condemning Derby to a sure-fire relegation.

Looking at his history a bit deeper and you'll see that he was no stranger to the role of goalkeeper. In fact, his nimble ability in this position proved to be a nice little earner for the Dubliner, as Jack Charlton would often recall.

Whilst on International duty, he would regularly make a few bob after training sessions challenging his team mates to penalties – whomever could score against him took the prize-money. However, the greater consequence of this financial side-line Charlton noted, was that it got the Irish team well-versed in the art of the penalty kick and was thought to be a contributing factor for their shoot-out victory over Romania during their Italia '90 campaign. After that, he became known as "Ireland's third 'keeper".

Like so many other occasions, all this seems to have been a pre-curser to his time at Sunderland, a club which he did everything for, except disappoint. That period, that team, will always be one that I personally use as a watermark for our future successes and it was that moment, I think, which sealed it for me. Ultimately, we all have Peter Reid to thank for bringing him to us in the first place and having faith in him after the six months he took off due to injury.

On the morning after that glorious Quinn-fuelled win over Bradford, I was walking into my high school in Northumberland. With a student base of over fifteen hundred and situated a mere twenty minutes north of Newcastle, I was only one of three fellow Sunderland supporters in the whole Mag-loving establishment. You can only imagine the stench but that morning I didn't mind it as much, though, as that day was a good one to be a Black Cat.

Thank you Niall – "Sunderland's third 'keeper!'"

Guy Galloway,

Seventy3 **Magazine writer.**

Originally taken from Seventy3 Magazine Issue 10.

"My main business involves selling polymers to convertors of plastic products, it involves a large amount of customer facing travel but naturally if I can combine this with Sunderland playing away on pre-season then it is a perfect trip as who doesn't like combining football, beer and expensing it?

I don't live on Wearside and since my father died in 2001 the trips have been less frequent. As a Sunderland supporter though I should go to many more games than I do but family and work does not always allow. Whenever the lads play away you may catch me singing my heart out or being asked to sit down as I do tend to get a bit over excited. The away games have always been exciting for me as the travelling support is hugely committed and passionate, even when going alone you are welcomed and accepted after wandering into heaving mass of Sunderland fans in that pub near the turnstiles. The shirt denotes I am one of this family and to be honest is probably still why I go to many more away trips than home games. I just love the atmosphere in the trenches away from home.

The seventh of August 2008 was the date I chose to visit Athlone Extrusions and I dragged along my old friend whom I work with in Eire, we all chatted over coffee and I kept a close eye on my watch as that very Thursday, purely by coincidence was the evening that Roy Keane's Sunderland team were to play a pre-season friendly at Athlone Town Stadium.

Now, my colleague for the trip, Peter Crerar is not a fan of football but using a few local contacts I had asked him to acquire two tickets for us to go. He knew I was a Sunderland fan but that evening he also undertook the journey in becoming one.

We left the appointment, checked into our hotel and set off for the stadium, me sporting my favourite Nike Replica shirt and very proud to be wearing it after a great season before. The excitement was building as I looked forward to seeing 1,000 travelling Mackems around the town. I was not disappointed, there was red and white everywhere en route to the ground. It's a single road that leads to the ground so we sat in traffic for about an hour before getting close enough to park, then we were on foot and joining the craic of Irish voices keen to see what the fuss was about with this man from Cork and his Premier League team visiting the middle of Ireland. This was my first chance to see the three man deal from Spurs with Malbranque, Tainio and Chimbonda rumoured to be playing alongside the numerous other fresh faces.

As we got closer to the crowd both Peter and I recognised a customer of ours, the owner of Mergon International just across the road and our paths were merging. We said hello and he asked us what we were doing here and I responded, well I was local so combined the trip, and then I noticed his tie. I asked where he got it and he replied, 'it's a Sunderland tie' and I said 'Yes, I know, I support them' to which the truth came out.

Despite years of doing business with his company and a few hellos in the corridors we had never discussed our personal lives, he now knew I was a huge Sunderland fan and I know knew that this same man, Pat Beirne had invested as part of the Drumaville Group. He was instrumental in getting my club to where they are today and I without this chat I may never have known just how instrumental. We left Pat to find our seats in the home end but he said to come and meet him at half-time for a cup of tea.

The first half was an easy 2–0 with goals from Richardson and Chopra but should have been more, this was an easy stroll for Sunderland and the fans were in good spirits. Then we left our seats in the packed little ground to find where to get this cup of tea.

Our names were on the door and we were greeted by Pat pouring us a drink, he was there relaxing with his friends and the conversation continued about how he got involved and why did I not speak with a Sunderland accent? He shared the master stroke of getting Keane to be the manager and how the Irish Sunderland family was growing rapidly and then he said 'I have someone for you to meet'. In comes this big man with a huge smile. I was now talking to Niall Quinn. I have no idea what I said but an impression was made as Niall invited Peter and I to join him for a drink at the local hotel that night.

The second half kicked off and we won 6–0, I can't recall the scorers or much of that half as all I could think about was meeting Niall again, playing over and over in my mind.

Now Peter thought this was all very funny, his gobby English friend being very nervous about a night out drinking - something I apparently do very well, mostly in his company I would say in my defence. He is now also assuming that every game of football the fans get to meet the owners of the club, this assumption is probably not helped by his other Sunderland game being also hospitality at the Stadium of Light... I really must stop treating him so much.

We got to the hotel around 8pm and there were a few Sunderland shirts about but we were guided to the rear of the bar and into a private section. Pat met us and again there was Niall. He came over to us and immediately asked what I thought of the game, my nerves were gone and he made us very comfortable. I offered to buy him a beer and so left to grab us some Guinness's. On returning he asked why I did not have the current shirt on, saying he needed support. I said it was a classic like him so we must celebrate the past as much as support the future, perhaps I have been destined to be involved in a retro magazine. The evening went far too quickly, I must say that Niall never bought me a drink back as promised nor did he give me a Directors tie as promised. If he approaches a bar people talk to him and he soon misses his place, so I doubt he ever gets a round in, a great strategy in saving money and key to managing a clubs finances I think.

He was working the room and left me with this young lad called Michael, he was amazingly passionate about the club, talked about his favourite players and who he wanted the team to buy for next season. He was very open and loved having the chance to meet another fan whom knew his favourite subject. This was Niall's son I was talking to and so proud to be a Sunderland fan.

I was privileged to spend over three hours with Niall and Michael and they were very open. Niall wanted to know what I did and suggested I join the Foundation of Light, I knew nothing of the charity arm for the club so said I would and still am a corporate member today having renewed for the fifth year.

As the night went on more people filled the lobby and bars and although no players were there the coaching staff were. Ricky Sbragia, Tony Coton, Tony Loughlan, all relaxing and talking to the fans. My club really was very open to mingling with the fans and I had never seen such an inclusive team, Niall really had impacted with his friendly and gregarious nature.

Well, then there was Roy Keane. He made an appearance and I got my picture taken with him. I am still not sure why but I am smiling and he is snarling at the camera, he was very pleasant though so perhaps my manners helped get that elusive picture as he rejected the chance to be seen with others.

Peter and I were buzzing, we went from attending a casual game to feeling like we played the match, we had exclusive VIP access to the owners based on a chance meeting with a customer whom we had no idea was involved in the club.

What a night!

I joined the Foundation very soon after and have met Niall a few times via this. The aim of the charity is to help the local area and 'give something back' but I would encourage everyone to join if capable as it enabled me to get close to some heroes of mine.

The horseracing at Sedgefield in 2009 was great as this was my first event and I got to meet some ex players. My hero is Marco Gabbiadini, he may not have been there but Eric Gates was, I grew up watching these guys play in the old third division and so to talk to him was a massive thrill for this middle aged guy. Who would have thought then I would make a career of stalking ex Sunderland players for *Seventy3* magazine? I think I am good at it, worryingly enough for the ex players that is.

Gordon Armstrong, John MacPhail shared stories of the past and even current players were there in Phil Bardsley, Anton Ferdinand and Kieran Richardson all there and happy to talk. They ran an auction and one prize was heavily competed for, at one stage my £1,000 bid was winning and I must admit to the nervousness at explaining this cost to my wife. But it could not cope with the strong demand and I recall the day racing with Niall at Cheltenham with first class travel and hotel went for over £3,000. It made me laugh that Niall described it as 'the plan is one day but if you are good fun it will probably turn into the whole three days festival package'. It was such a shame my pockets were not deep enough as that trip would be a chapter in itself!

I went to a few more Foundation events, they were limited as I live in London and when an infrequent attendee Niall always seemed to recognise me and say hello, he introduced me to then manager Steve Bruce one time and I chatted to this very friendly and likeable man, whom I can honestly say loved the club and wanted nothing more than success for Sunderland. His Geordie routes, for me, were in the eyes of a minority of fans and not the manager himself. His passion and desire for the club was clear, it is just a shame he never could turn that into tactical advantages on the pitch.

I cannot recall why but he gave me his personal number and for a few years I was able to text Niall with my support, on one occasion I told him I was to be at The Emirates on hospitality of an Arsenal fan. He said to call him and he would have a beer. I never expected him to be there but he was and he met me by a bar after the game.

The problem though is Niall is very popular and I doubt we finished a sentence without a request from the Arsenal fans for an autograph or a question. He never once seemed impatient or interrupted but was always very obliging. We shared a conversation around the passion of fans and he said he admired the likes of myself whom were unwavering in their positive approach to the club or team, yes I was disappointed for relegation or a loss but this would never deter me from feeling optimistic in the future. I made it clear to him my views and that is 'you can do whatever you want to my club and be sure that many are like me that no matter what, the club is assured of my support and I will always buy tickets to watch the lads, but never take it for granted'... he never did and I treasure the opportunity to have spent time with the great man that played, managed and ran my great club, Sunderland AFC."
Mark Harrison, *Seventy3* Magazine.

"Many images of Niall Quinn have been taken since he joined the club way back in 1996 when Peter Reid signed him from Manchester City but this is the one that will stick with me forever. It is the image used for the front cover of this book you have in your hands.

I was actually in this image before it was cropped as I made my journey down to the Stadium of Light front entrance to meet and greet the big man from Dublin. Maybe that's why it means so much to me that during one of the proudest moments of Quinn's football career

I was stood behind him in disbelief that he had become the new chairman of Sunderland AFC.

I remember the day well, there was massive media interest once they discovered that Quinny and his Drumaville Consortium brokered a deal to buy a stake in Sunderland AFC. Once the news broke that he would be down the Stadium of Light to be presented to the media my shoes and clothes were on halfway down the street. I met up with a few other friends to be a part of the magic that was being created in the boardroom. The walk down was a tough affair as the temperature was unknown in these parts of the world but a sign of a good day that lay ahead. I was amazed to get to the main entrance and see that we were not the only ones with this idea to see Quinny being announced as new Chairman of our football team.

The number of Sunderland fans continued to grow as rumours between the people, Internet and media began to escalate that he was about to be unveiled after discussions with the executives.

I will never forget the moment that the Irish striker that played 203 times in the red and white striped shirt came down in the lift and the whole crowd just stopped speaking. As though a Messiah was about to come and hand us bread and wine we waited with baited breath to make sure it really was him. Of course it was, you cannot miss him, and he is the tallest man I have ever seen in the flesh!

When he came outside into the glorious sunshine, which he probably called up and organised to appear on his big day, it was a sense of relief and optimism combined from everyone connected to the club. We were heading downwards at a very alarming rate and he was exactly what we needed to pull things together and move on as a strong club.

He took his time with everyone who had made the journey down to the Stadium of Light and entertained one crying child by simply smiling at her and this made her laugh immediately. A true sign of a man who is just gifted at being there at the right moment!

He spoke to the media just moments after this great snap was taken and we managed to hear everything that he said, as he had made a special speech to the fans along the same lines. His positive attitude and calm personality was a breath of fresh air from the usual drivel we heard from predecessors down the years that failed our team and management with indecisive actions.

The photographer who snapped this picture of the Irish striker who netted 61 times for Sunderland AFC also did something clever, maybe by accident?

Niall John Quinn or Sir Niall now, is seen to be holding his hands up in the sky in an act of celebration but where his hands are placed could be seen as significant in my opinion. The arms and hands are placed just under the right and left side of the Crest that is attached to the impressive West Stand and it looks as though he is holding up the club.

Very symbolic of what he aimed to do and what he has actually done for this club. He has held the club up from administration, brought in Roy Keane against all expectations, helped the club from bottom of the Championship into the Premiership on the first attempt. He then has kept our club in the top flight of English football for five consecutive seasons, something that has not been done in a long time, but more importantly he has turned us from being a "yo-yo" club into a strong team that now looks towards Europe.

Niall is a man of his word, and could quite possibly sell sand to the Arabs he has such a good way with people and the media. He envisaged a five year magic carpet ride and although we may have had some difficulties he just about delivered the targets we were all told back in June 2006.

Niall Quinn had a dream to take all the Sunderland fans on a magic carpet ride and for the majority of his tenure as chairman and major stakeholder the ride has been a very enjoyable one. A journey that I hope will continue so the carpet can take me to Europe to watch Europa league football and maybe even one day a

Champions League place amongst the elite, where Quinny belongs and hopefully can return to watch as a Sunderland fan.

They say every picture says a thousand words but this one will always say more to me for what he has done to help our club move forward."

Gary Johnson,

Seventy3 **Magazine writer.**

*Taken from Seventy3 Magazine Issue 3 and adapted for Magic Carpet Ride.

"Ellis Short has stepped into some huge shoes replacing Quinny and I sincerely hope he can continue the grand job that Niall has done at this club during his spell as club chairman.

Niall has taken this club to another level and we are rapidly becoming financially and globally a brand, something we were most definetly not, when he convinced Drumaville to take over.

He is a brilliant man and has done more for Sunderland football club than any other person. He is not only a great bloke, but a very dear friend of mine."

Bobby Kerr,

Sunderland AFC 1973 FA Cup winning Captain.

*Originally written for the Bobby Kerr column, Seventy3 Magazine, Issue 5.

"When you join a club, a big club like Sunderland you get to meet some great players. Looking around the dressing room that night when I first joined was Claudio Reyna, Kevin Phillips and Niall Quinn. You never know how people will react to you being the new player, the new face, voice and personality in the dressing room. All I can say was that Niall was a complete gentleman. He got on with his job and made everyone feel at home. When I joined he was struggling with a back injury and was probably only at 60%, but even then he was still a great player. I could only imagine what he was like to play with when 100% fit and not carrying a bad back.

He was a great representative of the club and a pleasure to play alongside."

Marcus Stewart, former team mate (and the player Quinn replaced as substitute in his final appearance in football – Sunderland v. West Ham United, Sunderland Stadium of Light, Saturday 19 October 2002.)

Sunderland AFC, 2002–2005.

"When he came to Manchester City myself and the likes of Garry Flitcroft would train with Quinny most of the time and helped work on his touch development. He was a big lad and he worked hard when he was at the club on this side of the game and he reaped the rewards.

Niall is a true gentleman of the game, was good with people of all ages and simply loved the game. It was very sad when he left City as a lot of people still felt he had a few years left in him yet and this was proved when he went to Sunderland and formed a superb partnership with Kevin Phillips.

He is held in high esteem everywhere he has been, especially at City. He did well for his country too under Jack Charlton and then Mick McCarthy for the Republic of Ireland.

Quinny though was a nightmare to go out with for a pint of Guinness. The man had no swallow and could knock back a pint of the black stuff no problem and a night out with the big fella was costly! The Guinness would just go down no problem and you could never keep pace with Niall.

I wasn't too surprised when he became chairman at Sunderland to be honest. He's that sort of bloke who can see both sides of a situation and it was something he turned his hand to. He did well in getting Roy Keane to the club and undoubtly Niall played a huge part in the club at Sunderland.

The book is a great idea and a tribute to Niall and I wish him all the best in the future."

Steve Lomas, former teammate,
Manchester City 1991–1997.

Tuesday, 22 August 2006. After a dismal opening 80 minutes against lowly Bury, Sunderland collapse and concede two late goals, meaning we lose this cup game against the side sat at the very foot of the bottom division of the football league.

Along with four straight league defeats, the club are in complete despair – and with 1,200 deeply concerned away fans on his back, Sir Niall Quinn promises he will step down as manager and find a world class replacement within a week.

Fast forward just over six years and we are an established Premier League side with a very healthy bank balance and mid table finishes just behind us. Words simply cannot describe what the man has done for us – after all, without him we could be in the same shape that 'big' sides like Sheffield United are in at present. We'd probably be playing away at sides like Stevenage and Yeovil, still paying off debts owed for Tore Andre Flo, still in a rut. Without Niall Quinn, the Drumaville revolution would not have happened, we'd never have acquired a name like Roy Keane (even if untried at managerial level) on board and without the Saint of Dublin, we'd never have a Billionaire Texan keeping us affloat.

Quinn saved us from the brink of crisis. He didn't have to – but he did. He made us fashionable again. Off his own back, he saw where we were headed and convinced a group of wealthy businessmen that backing a club in freefall was a good investment. He sold them all the Sunderland dream – the dream of one day becoming successful. He told them of our passion, our never-say-die attitude that we demand from our players, and he told them of his love for the club that gave him his second chance, his Indian summer. He wanted to give the fans a second chance too – a chance to stand up and stop being embarrassed of who we had become.

It still amazes me. Why did he do it? What made him suddenly decide that he was going to leave his cushy life as an analyst on TV, to roll up his sleeves and work his arse off to take the club from the brink of despair into a new era? It's a love story, the kind you rarely hear of in football. Pure and simple, Niall Quinn loves Sunderland AFC and will never stop loving it. Without sounding cliched, if you cut him open he'd bleed red and white.

Where did the love story begin? This club gave Niall Quinn a second chance when nobody else would have him. Various doctors had told him he was finished as a professional footballer and that it was about time to pack in. The media thought it, the footballing world thought it – he was done.

Then out of nowhere, Peter Reid plucked a certain lofty Irish centre-forward from Man City. Not long after signing, Quinny's knee gave way, great we thought, we'd spent money on a carthorse!

The following season he met Kevin Phillips and the rest they say is history. The fans loved him, his team mates loved him, but most importantly he felt wanted again, he'd found his home.

Fast forward through time and Quinny is at the club as Chairman. What might have happened had Niall not come in still makes me shudder. Even though he has stepped aside, he has left the club in capable hands in Ellis Short. I for one truly believe, Niall would not just hand over control to anyone, he clearly believes Mr Short can go on to take the club to the next level. As Sir Niall is a people person, he perhaps then is not ruthless enough to make the tough decisions, that Mr Short is accustomed to.

We are now unrecognisable as a club from what we were and this is down to a lot of people's hard work, none more though than Mr Quinn.

Rome though wasn't built in a day and so remember this, when venting your frustration on message boards, social networking sites, in the pub, or with your mates in the stands, consider that although things do not look particularly rosy we are bloody lucky that once upon a time an Irishman with a kind heart took us in and made us what we are today.

Thank you Niall Quinn for saving club – you will forever be regarded as the saviour of Sunderland AFC.

Gavin Henderson, Former Online Editor,

Seventy3 **Magazine.**

Taken from Seventy3 Magazine, Issue 5 and edited and adapted for Magic Carpet Ride.

"Well it wasn't all plain sailing was it? When he first arrived as a player he wasn't 100% fit and he did get some stick as life at Roker Park did not start smoothly.

I think it would be fair to say some sections of the crowd thought Reidy may have made a costly mistake, £1.3 million to be precise, for a player past his best who was on the treatment table while the lads slipped out of the top tier in 1997. Thankfully for us, those doubters (me included if I'm honest) couldn't have been more wrong – it was just the start of Quinny's love affair with the greatest team in the land. His never-to-be-forgotten telepathic partnership with Super Kevin Phillips will be talked about from generation to generation as argu-ably SAFC's most potent-ever strikeforce. Even when he'd hung up his boots, he was not finished, the magic carpet ride began and - ignoring his brief, and awful, effort at management - he has helped take the club to another level.

We have Bob Murray to thank for our fantastic stadium (still not best pleased with its name mind) but we have Big Niall to thank for putting Sunderland AFC firmly on the worldwide map of football. He and Drumaville had a great vision. The club has been sold to football fans all over the world with a huge fanbase now out in Africa. Chair-man Ellis Short an astute businessman and now, I hear, a huge fan of English football and SAFC in particular was sold Niall's vision. He and the rest of the forward-thinking management side of the club continue to lead the club into new ventures. Who'd have thought we'd have our 'home' hosting concerts such as Rihanna, Coldplay, Take That and… Bon Jovi. Just those names show how far our club has come and I believe it is down to Quinny finding the right people who have really bought in to the passion of SAFC. The club is on a sounder footing as I can ever remember – we just need the players to perform now.

I can't think of too many mistakes made in Quinny's time at the club. His handful of games in charge as manager has perhaps told him his future is in the media, rather than in the dugout! He could have also perhaps mentioned to a couple of managers that Darryl Murphy, try as he might, was not a good enough forward to be playing for

SAFC either. Other than that, I think Niall has a clean bill of health.

The man is a legend and it is hardly surprising he is still revered at Arsenal, Manchester City and Sunderland. It is difficult to say a bad word about him and if we could keep him on the club's roll of honour so to speak, we should make it happen.

I was lucky enough to interview the great man himself while he was still playing for Sunderland. I was working on a golf magazine when I nabbed the job for myself (no-one else was going to do this interview) and we fixed up a day for me to go and interview him out on the golf course at Wynard down the A19. It is fair to say that with my agricultural golf swing and erratic putting I was petrified of looking like a massive fool so it was perhaps with a sense of relief that Quinny rang me to say he was carrying a knock and that an interview up at the old Whitburn training ground would be preferable.

So up I drove, waved through the gates by security, passing the hoardes of fans watching the lads training. Back in those days, the facilities were pretty much a row of Portakabins. No sooner had I got out of my car and wandering around between players I idolise on a weekend (including a brief sighting of the lesser spotted Milton Nunez), Quinny takes an educated guess and shouts me over and offers me a cup of tea.

Now at this point I could have turned into a jibbering, unprofessional mess, but I held it together as I spent half an hour or so (which flew by) in the company of a man so eloquent and so passionate about the club I probably should have realised back then (the year 2000) that he'd probably end up having such an important role in the development of our club.

It was a pleasure to meet him and interview him and is the undoubted highlight of my 18-odd years in journalism. I sent him a copy of the magazine and got him to sign a copy of the interview for me, which still hangs proudly on my wall at home. What a man!

One can only imagine how much fun the big fella is over 10 pints of Guinness (while wearing his disco pants of course)."

Jon Stokoe, Former Editor,
Whitby Gazette.

In an interview especially for this book, we thought it apt to catch up with Niall's former Marketing and Commercial Director – Lesley Callaghan, who was also performing the same role when he arrived as a player in 1996.

What was Niall Quinn like to work with?

"Niall was full of energy and ideas but also happy to let us get on with the job. As a player he always did more than his fair share from press interviews to public appearances and as Chairman was a charismatic figure head."

How exciting was it when he came back to Sunderland in 2006?

"I was aware that Niall had spoken to Bob Murray (then Sunderland Chairman) some time before and had been interested in investing in the club, and that Bob had suggested he should take a bigger role.

The sale of the club and finding the right new owner was a huge responsibility for the Board. We were in the advanced stages of due diligence with another potential American buyer when Niall suddenly reappeared and announced he'd managed to put together a consortium.

Our focus changed quickly because passing the club to someone who knew what it stood for and understood its history and its importance to the city and the region was exciting.

Working with Drumaville was great fun. It wasn't the most structured time but they all got involved with the club for the right reason because they loved sport and wanted to win like the fans."

Niall's legacy?

"Bob built the Stadium, the Academy and the club back up from the lows of 8,000 at Roker Park to 48,000 at the SOL.

We were at a low point in football terms in 2006 and with the return of Niall and his inspired appointment of Roy Keane we became, in his words "Box Office" again. He reignited interest, belief and excitement and re-connected with the fans."

Interesting stories about Mr. Quinn?

"Let me see, there are so many but not all of them can be printed!

The fact that he had me pitch for the club's top sponsorship to Boylesports at Cheltenham - not in the private suite he promised but something that resembled a stair well! And he forgot to get us any passes to get in...

The night he called me from Bristol Airport and asked me to get him some coaches after the Cardiff match and then proceeded to order a fleet a taxis to bring everyone home – but had no money! My husband, brother-in-law and others then emptied the cash points at Bristol airport!

His eclectic boardroom guest list which one week might include International sports stars and the next priests and dentists – many of which he didn't remember inviting and most of which he had forgotten to tell us about!

But overall I remember his sense of fun and "fair play" as the Irish love to say."

Lesley was speaking to *Seventy3's* Mal Robinson.

"I had the honour of opening this book and had the chance to close it, however I will leave that to the man himself with one of his all time classic quotes, which has now been immortalised into Wearside folklore.

Before I do that though I would like one final word on the big fella. As you can see from all that has gone before us in this publicaton alone, Niall Quinn has been the most important man in our recent history.

Even in every issue of *Seventy3* (and there have been 15 issues to date) Niall has appeared in some form or the other, be it from former colleagues, or fans alike, and not a bad word has been written.

I remember the day Roy Keane walked away from Sunderland and three subsequent managers since. On each occasion, the fans moved on, as football and life in general has a habit of doing, you must that is just the way it is. Time stands still for no man.

Yet when the news filtered through of Niall Quinn's departure from Sunderland AFC, it was like a relative had passed away and I think a little chink of Irish charm, emblazoned in red and white colours died that day and has had a lasting effect, even if only in the subconscious of the club and its people. The days when a happy go lucky Irishman who once paid for a fleet of taxis for stricken fans may be over, he may label Sunderland as 'them' and not 'us' these days, but Niall Quinn, the player, the manager and the chairman, will never be forgotten by Sunderland fans across the globe.

James Allan may have founded Sunderland and District Teachers Assocaition Football Club in 1879, yet it was another Celt by the name of Quinn, whom 127 years later ensured Allan's inception stood firm into the modern digital age, the aim of being Sunderland 'til we die, for many generations to come.

Take it away, Niall."

Malcolm Robinson, Editor in Chief,
Seventy3 **Magazine and** *The Red & White Lite.*

"I learned my trade at Arsenal, became a footballer at Manchester City, but Sunderland got under my skin... I love Sunderland".

Niall Quinn, former player, manager and chairman.
Sunderland AFC 1996–2002 and 2006–2012.

Thanks and Acknowledgements

I would like to thank the following for helping make this project become a reality. Thanks to the writing team of Jim Fox, Gary Johnson, Gary Emmerson, Chris Siddell, Stephen Linsley, Andrew Powell, Kelly Leigh Cooper and Gavin Callaghan. Also to Andrew Brewster for the design work on the jacket. Graham Halliday for the monumental proof reading – a thankless task.

Thanks also go to Mark Harrison, Nathan Johnson and the team at Sunderland World, Gavin Henderson, Guy Galloway, Richard Holt from PA photos for his advice, former players and team mates – Kevin Phillips for putting his name to and producing an apt foreword for the big man, Micky Gray, Thomas Sorensen, Marcus Stewart, Steve Lomas, Jody Craddock and Gavin McCann. Everyone at the *Sunderland Echo* for their help and support, all the media and press guys, Gary Johnson hounded for his chapter!

To anyone else we have missed off this list, you know who you are – so thanks!

Thanks also to Sunderland AFC for their help and advice on the book and to Steven Caron for his patience at DB publishing.

Mal Robinson.
www.seventy3magazine.co.uk
www.redandwhitelite.co.uk

References and Resources

BBC Breakfast with Frost
BBC Five Live
BBC Sport
Northern Echo
Seventy3 Magazine
Sky Sports News
Sunderland Echo
The Guardian
The Journal
The Stat Cat
Wikipedia
Magic Carpet Ride